Lucky Penny

A Novel of

Self Discovery

By

Richard Gallup

This is a book of fiction. The characters within are not intended to represent any actual people, living or dead.

Lucky Penny

Like a lucky penny,
I found Northwood
and stayed there a while.

It was a warm blanket on my bed
in winter.
An umbrella held close
in stormy weather.
It was a friendly scratch on the back
that found just the right spot.

And after a lifetime of other places,
Northwood stays with me.
A delicate flower
pressed in the pages
of an old book
that brings a smile to my face
and a tear to my eye.

It was just a lucky penny
found unexpectedly,
but I will forever hold it
in my pocket.

The Moment

Everything started in 1975 with a phone call to an old friend I hadn't spoken to in years and didn't then. His wife answered and I knew her voice. It was Lynne, that pretty girl with long hair, who sat behind me in senior English.

My high school remembrances are not about the prom, homecoming, the class play, etc. I avoided all those things. I didn't want to participate in sports pep rallies either, but fortunately there was a study hall option on those occasions, supervised by Mr. *Narcolepsy,* an equally apathetic teacher. I'd see Lynne there.

One day near the end of the year, I was particularly upset waiting in line at the lunchroom, thinking about how I might avoid conscription into the armed forces. Viet Nam loomed in my future. Everyone around me was chattering gaily about stupid trivial things. The prom? Really? Didn't these people know the world was exploding with war, starvation, and global environmental disasters? I didn't know what a panic attack was, but started to have one, not my first. My heart pounded in my chest, I shook all over, a sweat was soaking my hair, and I couldn't breathe! I had to get outside, right now! I hurried down the hall and out the front doors of the school, holding onto one of the pillars, panting. The beautiful spring day and a couple slow deep cleansing breaths calmed me down quickly, but then I saw I was not alone. Another escapee for reasons different from my own, Lynne, was sitting on the steps with her head in her hands. I sat down beside her. After a brief silence, we shared our woes with each other in a bonding moment.

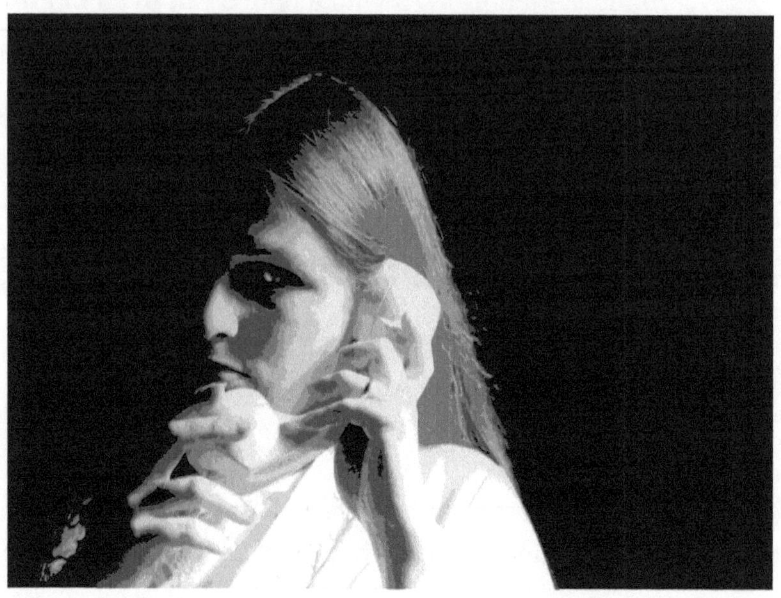

Several years later, there was her voice on the phone, my fellow misfit schoolmate. As we chatted, I sensed her path still had plenty of ups and downs and felt sad.

"And you, Rick?" she asked, "Are you happy?"

The question stumped me. Happy!? I never thought of life in terms of happiness and wasn't sure I knew what happiness meant. But the moment she asked that question was the moment the long process began.

The Boys

Before we all had computers, social networking was face to face. You met someone you got along with and became friends, and then you slowly got acquainted with *their* friends. One of them would show up with their brother, who shared an interest with you, and a week later you connected with *his* circle. On a city bus, you'd run into a fellow who sat next to you in a class at the university and invite him to an informal gathering at your house on Saturday. "Bring a friend," you'd say. You didn't have to be particularly gregarious to experience this ever-widening sphere of influence. You just had to be open to it.

That was me in the mid-1970s of Columbus, Ohio. I was a rudderless ship, going with the ebb and flow of tide surrounding me. Instead of participating, I hid behind my camera, visually recording everything and everyone. A couple times a week, I developed film and made prints in a makeshift darkroom I put together in the basement of my apartment. More or less by accident, I acquired a halfway decent job that utilized those skills. Life sort of rolled along for me.

I met Arthur at a random gathering at my place initiated by my wife of several years. She was by far the more social one in our relationship. There were three of us hiding out in the kitchen from the party, interested in playing cards, so I walked around the house to find a fourth for Bridge, not everyone's game. I found Art, wall-flowering in the living room, and he joined us as my partner and turned out to be a sharp, experienced player. I also saw that he was a sane, down to earth person with a plan in life. Unlike myself, but, somehow, the sort I'm drawn to.

After the game we talked about my photography, while I tried to build a house of cards, symbolic of my life. There were photos of mine in every room of the apartment and Art asked me about my process and philosophy. "My what?!" I tried to explain to him, and to myself, that I had neither, but went about photography intuitively, like I did everything else.

"I need a passport photo," he said, "and I think it would be fun to have a creative one. I read that anything goes, as long as the face is clearly visible and represents the person well." He raised one eyebrow. "Maybe you'd be interested in helping me." It could have been the flattery, but I volunteered to get together with him in the morning for a shoot.

Art lived on Northwood, a pleasant, tree-lined street that rose steadily away from High Street at the edge of Ohio State University. Residents were largely older students, graduate students, and former students who found themselves still living there twenty years after leaving school. A couple blocks up the hill, Art shared a house with Wayne and Max, his high school classmates and fellow university students.

Max was an outdoorsy nature boy, with a rough red beard and crazed look in his eyes, who laughed a little too easily and loudly. His lows seemed pretty low, too. I watched him cautiously, like a wild animal off the leash. His major was something about environmental sciences or natural resources. On weekends, he was likely to be out in the woods somewhere. When I met him, he was lining up a summer job in a national park.

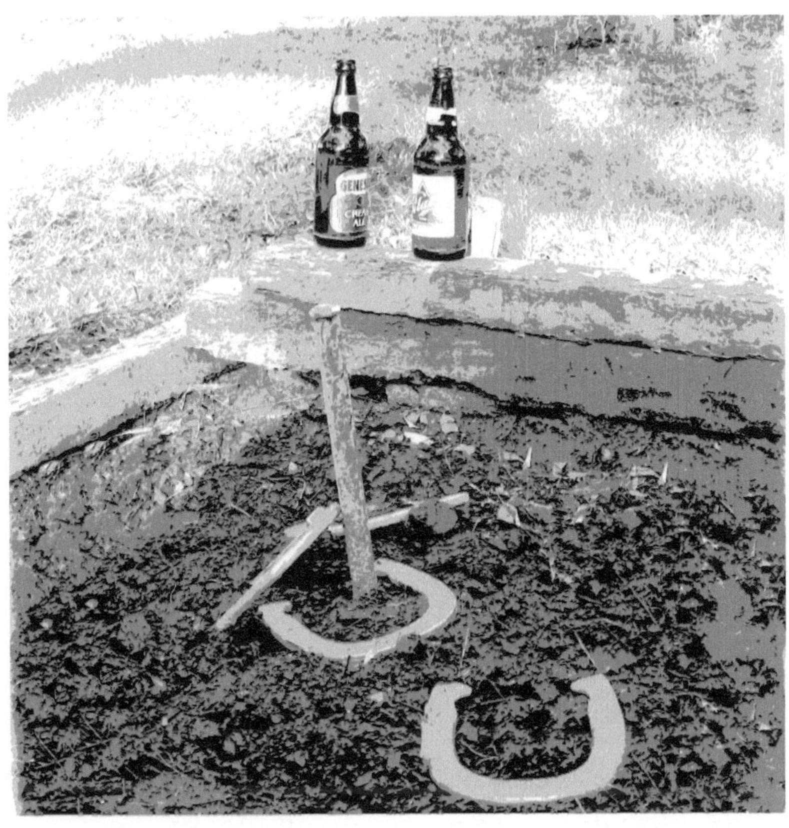

Wayne, an animal lover, was trying very hard to get into the universities' prestigious veterinary school, and taking classes to help him in that direction. Despite the stressful education plans, his demeanor was as calm as Buddha, perhaps partly due to the ever-present dab of tobacco in his cheek. He was the shortest of the three, but sturdily built with a big heart, ready to offer a helping hand wherever needed.

Art was in the architectural school, his room dominated by a large drawing table in those pre-personal computer days. He was quite intellectual with a broad range of interests. His mild wild side emerged when he climbed on his motorcycle. This was a mid-sized get around town bike, but the eyes behind the mirrored, *Easy Rider* shades saw it as a monster, cross-country road hog. It made him feel free. My passport photo of him was his reflection in the bike's mirror with the edge of his hand on the throttle visible.

A frequently used horseshoe court stretched out along the side of the house. Many an amiable gathering of neighbors occurred in this yard and house. They seemed to know most everyone on that end of the street, where they were affectionately known as The Boys. But let me back up a bit and begin once more.

Hello, Columbus

Acceptance to Ohio State University as a freshman brought me to Columbus, Ohio in 1971. I had no distinct education plan or view of the future, other than my strong desire not to die for my country. Choosing whatever courses struck my fancy, I faithfully got up every morning and went to class. Freshmen at OSU had boring 101 introductory classes in auditoriums with a few hundred fellow students. The curriculums were not particularly interesting, but prerequisite for any field of study. Some of these mega-classes were taught by a teacher on television screens hanging down all around the hall. In an early version of *hacking*, I carefully doctored my computer punch card with a razor blade and tiny pieces of tape, and became a sophomore, allowing me to make more focused excursions into history, philosophy, art, and music. I also took some psychology, to see if I could get a clue about why I was so uncomfortable in the world. It didn't offer any help, because I identified with *every* clinical version of craziness in the textbook.

Freshmen are required to live in a dormitory, *no thank you*, if not living with family. My recently graduated jerk of a brother was about to leave Columbus, and agreed to go to the housing office and say I was living with him. Then I took over his apartment and shared it with the brother of my girlfriend, who was at Kent State University. The brother was a senior and in love with my older sister, who practically moved in with us. The two of them were the opposite of me in temperament, world view, religiosity, and politics. They were nattily attired young Republican Christians.

The University community, in contrast, was beyond liberal at the time. All the clichéd trappings of hippydom were very real and everywhere: long hair, bell-bottoms, and pot smoked openly. On campus and on High Street, along the edge of campus, anti-war protests seemed never-ending. I wasn't closely involved with the movement, but joined in when opportunity arose. The elected student body president was a full-bearded Jewish leftist who wanted to turn the campus upside-down. There were still preppy frat guys in suits and ties, but they were definitely the odd ones.

The billiard room in the basement of the student union was my regular escape. As you walked in the front door, there was a very wide staircase to the lower level with a shiny hardwood banister in the middle. I was there so often, it became second nature to fly in the door, plop side-saddle on the banister and slide down, jumping off just before the bottom step, and landing on my feet with a whole lot of forward momentum. Once I slammed into Coach Woody Hayes, like a brick wall, who was walking fast along the lower hallway. He brushed me off like a mosquito, unamused.

Playing eight ball was a quiet peaceful escape for me, erasing stress and worry for an hour or so. It also fed my need to hone skills with my hands. I liked using my hands, and becoming the best I could be at things, like playing guitar and making artsy crafty things, though never considering them avenues to making a living. When my hands learned a complicated skill, a confidence arose in my body and, in turn, my mind. At the end of my days, I returned to the apartment to find young *Ozzie & Harriet* studying together or playing kissy-face in the living area/bedroom. The bathroom was not much larger than what you find on an airplane, but served its purpose. The only other room was the kitchen, where I could do my reading or studying in peace, occasionally pausing to smash cockroaches, which were ubiquitous throughout the south campus student slums.

Then came a day circled on my calendar: the first military draft lottery. Each day of the year and leap year were put in a hopper in Washington and mixed up. One by one, the dates were drawn to determine who would be drafted to replenish our armed forces, dropping dead before our eyes on the evening news. I was in a lounge at the student union after class listening to the radio, all the seats taken and hard to find an empty spot on the floor. It was already underway, but I didn't see my birthday on the list being made on a large pad. Groaning and cursing arose in the early going, as the crowd slowly thinned out. When my birthday finally was called, I was lying on my back with an arm over my eyes. It was number 273. I wept. The heavy weight was lifted, and I would not die for my country or escape to Canada after all. I started to feel light on my feet as I walked back to the apartment. I skipped, jumped, and spun around as I went along, singing *Goodbye Columbus*. But I didn't leave Columbus.

Against her parents' wishes, my girlfriend married me and transferred to OSU. We were nineteen. The four years we were together is a subject I could also write a book about, but would rather forget. Were we happy? We experienced the *entire* cycle of emotions, from pre-soak to spin and through the ringer. Infatuated and inseparable at first, but that didn't last long. Trying to get along came next, followed by throwing things at each other. Was that how most marriages worked?

"It's not that I don't love you, Rick," she said, as our relationship circled the drain, "It's just that I want to have sex with other men." She was a liberated woman and wanted us to have an *open* relationship. After all we'd been through, there didn't seem to be much left to feel. She said she was confused and needed some time alone to sort things out, suggesting a trial separation. I put clothes in my backpack, walked ten blocks south, knocked on Arthur's door, and asked for a night on his sofa. Max left that morning for his summer job at Olympic National Park, so Art and Wayne invited me to live in his room for the summer. That's how I became, for a while, one of The Boys.

Signs

Ten blocks in another direction from Northwood there was a sign company where I was employed. I was primarily the photography-silk screen printing department, but was occasionally put to work lettering trucks or large signs with an oil brush. Water-based tempera lettering, called *showcard*, being more difficult, was done by employees with much more skill and experience than I possessed at the time.

Although I enjoyed the work and was learning a lot, there were reasons for feeling stressful there. Some jobs had a promised deadline looming, causing everyone to work at a faster than comfortable pace. Like most any workplace, a project requiring teamwork brought out personality conflicts.

Both my employer's sons worked at the place, neither particularly suited for the job. They didn't get along with each other very well either, always bickering or trying to make each other look bad in front of 'the old man'. When I first started there, they totally ignored me, which was better than they treated some employees. Fortunately, they were out half the time, delivering and erecting signs or picking up supplies.

Not long after moving in with The Boys on Northwood, I started work with my head in a funk and was immediately sent out with The Brothers on a complicated sign erection. Sitting between them in the cab of the pickup did little to dispel my gloomy mood. I kept my attention on the road ahead and soon noticed my old neighborhood all around us.

This was not my first adventure with The Brothers, so I wasn't surprised when they suggested stopping somewhere for breakfast. While away from the shop, they were never in a big hurry to accomplish anything. I suggested Marie's Diner, a place my wife and I frequented at the corner of Weber and High. I knew the waitress standing at the cash register in a lacy apron as we walked in. Recognizing me, she pointed with raised eyebrows and gestured with the menus in her hand. In a cozy back nook sat my wife having *breakfast* with some guy, his arm around her. Dishes clattering and the din of voices filled my head. I mumbled something and stumbled back out to the street, hugging the stop sign for support. There was something left to feel after all.

The Brothers attitude toward me completely changed after the incident at Marie's. "Are you going to kill her?" one of them asked? "I'd kill her!" The other nodded and said he knew where I could get a hot gun. I enjoyed their sudden acknowledgement of my existence and didn't want to argue with them. They were the sort of people you'd rather get along with. After a while, they also started to respect me for my photography and screen printing skills back at the shop. Once, I ran into one of them at a restaurant with his girlfriend, and he warmly greeted me. Relationships evolve.

The Volcano

At The Boys house, I all but quit eating for a while, and though I continued to take in fluids, they mostly contained alcohol. Arthur and Wayne were both understanding and kind, but also avoided me when I was blubbering in my beer. This wasn't like the *Dear John* high school break-ups of my past. The painfully abrupt end of a four-year marriage isn't something you can put behind you overnight.

Before the split, my wife and I started relationship counseling. The therapist was Mary McSomething, but I called her Mary McFreud. She smiled, but gave me a penetrating look over the rim of her spectacles. Counseling was my idea. I thought my partner was going through a difficult time and had some things she needed to work out. After all, I was the devoted, monogamous spouse.

The surprise, at least for me, was that I turned out to be the one with deep, unresolved, psychological issues. It was obvious from the first session. Yes, I took a lot of abuse as a child from a much older brother. No, it wasn't just the draft lottery that led me to drop out of the university. I was an anonymous number on the big campus, yet I had panic attacks whenever I was called on to participate overtly in a class.

My parents were unsettled when I was small and moved a lot, causing me to attend five different schools before starting the second grade. They were east coast, west coast, rural and big city. School was a nightmare, but when I wasn't there, I was running from my brother, who thought it was great fun to hold me down and torture me.

After that first visit with Mary, I realized I was angry. I thought I was confused and concerned about my wife, but then I had a vision of myself actually killing her! Seeing that I was a volcano about to explode, threw me into a full-blown anxiety reaction. Think about it. What would happen to me if I lost it and really strangled her? You read stories like that in the newspaper all the time. I took myself to the emergency mental health clinic, where I was given a prescription and an immediate dose of a very effective calming medication, which put a temporary cork in the volcano. I continued to see Mary by myself after that. She would help me excavate the mountain slowly and safely, or so I hoped.

My life started moving forward. Working at the sign shop gave me a feeling of self-worth. Many life lessons would be found there. In my new neighborhood, my natural inclination would have been to go about my way quietly. That end of Northwood was a friendly, busy place, though, and I was drawn into the community as if an invisible hand guided me. There were many evening get-togethers and barbecues. Some Saturday afternoons, we had friendly softball games at a nearby park with another neighborhood a few streets away. It was a stroke of luck to find myself in a great place to nurse my wounds and start over.

Life Coach

Stepping out on the front porch of The Boys house early Saturday morning, I saw a short, mustachioed guy sipping a mug of coffee on the porch across the street. He looked familiar and, after a minute, I remembered him, a friend of a friend of a friend.

At Kent State, my fiancée's roommate, Hazel's boyfriend, Jacob, had an uncle who owned a very old, historic log cabin on the square in Zoar village. Zoar, Ohio is kind of a mini Williamsburg, with lots of exhibits and tour guides in period attire. Jacob and Hazel invited a bunch of people to hang out at the family cabin for the weekend. When I look at my old photos, I see us frolicking in the yard while tourists and 18th century impersonators walked by, trying to ignore us.

We met Dan and Lulu there, who happened to move into an apartment a few doors from us on Hudson Street a couple years later. We were at their place one evening, when this short guy in a suit stumbled in with a pint of scotch in his hand. "Everything to excess," he toasted us and took a hit off the bottle. Dan introduced his brother, Sid, with some embarrassment. I could tell Sid wasn't as sloshed as he made himself look. Dan was a medical student and frowned upon excess. There was some kind of sibling dynamic at work. I know something about those.

So there was Sid, living directly across the street from The Boys. He pointed at me, looked down, and scratched his chin. By the time I crossed and started climbing the steps to his porch, he had it, pointing at me again. "Rick," he said, "Hudson Street. I heard there was a new face over there. But you? You with the beautiful wife?"

"Soon to be ex-wife," I said. I gave him the Cliff Notes version of my saga.

"You need to go out and get laid, young man," he said with authority.

While we talked, he picked up a watering can and gave the various potted plants a drink. I noticed the yard and house were very well cared for. "Coffee?" he asked after watering. "Come on in." Sid's apartment was the bottom half of the house. As I walked in, I saw that his place was neat and tidy. A very good quality folk guitar leaned in the corner. Well framed art prints hung on the walls and more potted plants sat by the windows. Sid was working on his doctorate in psychology at that point in his life. His brother, Dan, intended to pursue psychiatry after med school. I wondered if there was madness in their family to draw them both to mental health fields.

Sid also worked part-time, counseling at a substance abuse clinic. That surprised me at first, knowing he enjoyed good scotch, but he had seen enough lives ruined by booze to be wary of over-doing it himself.

Over the next few weeks, I saw there was one addiction he was a slave to. The man wanted sex all the time and with a variety of partners. He had several girlfriends at any given moment. Most of them only lasted a couple weeks.

"Women want to kiss you with that broom on your lip?" I asked?

"I use a softener on it," he said, "It tickles them when I dive the muff."

"Dive?" I asked, "Pardon me?"

"Young man," he said, "You are in need of guidance."

I could see his lifestyle could be problematic, but I thought some of his skills would be nice to have. I had to admire the ease with which he found willing partners. We became good friends, so I got to see him in action sometimes and probed him about technique. "It's the easiest thing in the world," he would say. Even with his good advice, I found meeting strange women painful. "They're only strangers for a minute," he said like a mantra. In general, my life was a complete mess compared to his neat and ordered existence and ability to get what he wanted. I listened carefully to his advice and started calling him my life coach for a little joke. Sid smiled and wore the title with pride.

Closure

The resurrection of my marriage fell off my list of possibilities for the future. That fact mostly stabbed my heart, but at the same time, a vague sense of liberation crept in. On the practical side, I left behind stuff I needed, and she had our car. Sid offered to drive and give me a hand, when we were sure she wasn't home. Thanks, Sid.

It felt spooky walking into the apartment we shared, but I tried to concentrate on what I needed: the rest of my clothes, some books and records, photo and darkroom equipment, and my toolbox. If life is measured by belongings, mine didn't amount to a very big pile of stuff. It all fit easily into Sid's little car.

We were finished and about to go, when I thought I forgot something. We went back inside and I looked around for pencil and paper. I wrote a short spontaneous poem, with Sid reading beside me.

"Do what you must," he said, "But closure is what you need most."

"It hurts," I said, "Writing a poem is sort of who I am." I took the key off my ring and left it on the poem.

Sid saw the tears in my eyes and put a hand on my shoulder, as we locked the door behind us. "Trust me, Bro," he said, "In six months everything will look different."

Camera Man

Karl, a blond, blue-eyed, giant of a man, lived in the second floor and finished attic above Sid. We hit it off right away, because he was a photographer and worked in the photo section of the Lazarus department store downtown. His camera of choice was a medium format two and a quarter twin lens reflex and he, too, had a make-shift darkroom. We never ran out of photophilic issues to discuss and went on shoots together a couple times.

Karl had been through his share of break-ups, and empathized with the changes in my life. He was good with words and often had just the right turn of phrase to take the edge off my pain and anger. Inside the large frame was a sensitive, gentle soul. And he was gay.

Shortly after we met, he wanted to tell me he was gay, breaking it to me softly, like I might be offended. I wasn't, and, in fact, had the impression Karl *was* gay. Sid told me he would invite me up to his kitchen for coffee and a chat about it. I liked the big galoot, and being gay was clearly a sensitive issue for him. He wanted me to know he was a mature, conservative gay person and not a part of the crazy, flamboyant, limp-wristed crowd.

While we sipped coffee and talked, I closely examined the artwork on his kitchen walls, like I do everywhere. When the opportunity to segue came, I pointed to a little etching. "I know this artist!" I said, "Where did you get that?"

"I bought that at the student art sale on campus," he said, "Maybe, ten years ago. Tell me about her."

I launched into a story, starting with a small circle. Sarah was my brother's girlfriend's schoolmate from Cleveland. He only met her once, but she happened to move into an apartment near him and they became friends. I was visiting my brother at OSU for a few days when I was in high school, but he didn't have a lot of time for me, busy schedule and whatever. Sarah saw what was going on and took me under her wing, showing me around campus and High Street, and feeding me at her place. Thanks, Sarah.

She was a graduate student in the visual arts college, so I got a thorough tour of those classrooms and facilities. My enthusiasm for that led her to invite me to her seminar with the arts department chairman. "This man is like the Holy Father of art," she whispered to me, as we took our seats among the circle of chairs in his classroom. While we waited for the professor to arrive, I noticed nervousness in the other students. "He might not like my bringing you," Sarah warned me, quietly.

When the revered man came in, there was absolute silence. He took a seat in the circle and spent a long couple minutes looking at each one of us, stopping at me. "How old are you, young man?" he asked me softly, "And why are you in my seminar?"

"Fifteen, sir," I answered, "My name is Rick, and I'm a friend of Sarah's from Cleveland."

"Tell me, Rick," he asked, smiling, "Are you an artist?"

The question surprised me, but I didn't hesitate. "Yes, sir," I said. "I am an artist."

"I believe you," he said, with kindness in his eyes, "You may stay."

The professor set a tiny table in the center of the circle. Then he took out his neatly folded handkerchief and laid it there. "To understand the handkerchief, you draw it like this." he began. "Then you draw it like this." He flipped it partly open. "And this." He opened it more and let a corner hang over the edge of the table. "And then this, this, and this." He moved it one way and another. "And you draw it a hundred different ways. When you are done, you will *own* the handkerchief!" he said dramatically, pulling the cloth to his chest. "Then whenever it is called for, the handkerchief is at the tip of your pencil, chalk, or brush."

He said nothing after that for a few minutes, letting his words sink in. Then he continued, pausing between each thought. "Being an artist is not a gift. No one is born with talent. You must have immense desire, knowledge, and experience to be an artist." He put his hands together as if in prayer. "Above all," he said, "Art comes from dedication and very hard work." The seminar didn't last a long time, but its message hit me hard.

"Sorry to go on," I said, continuing in a much lighter tone, "but that was the moment I knew I'd spend my life in the artsy-fartsy world."

"Don't apologize," Karl said, "That was fascinating. I'll never look at that etching the same way again." He took it off the wall and held it. "You know, I can see how the prof's lesson relates to photography."

"To any of the arts," I said.

"But when the two of us photograph something, our negatives are very different!" he said.

"Sure. There are an *infinite* number of ways to photograph something," I said.

"And now I'm thinking," he said with a smile, "there are an infinite number of ways to approach love and life."

"Yeah, well," I said, "That's a whole hell of a lot of hard God damn work, too!"

Welcome

Maybe it happened all over America every day, but a neighborhood where everybody got along and even liked each other was something new for me. Much of my childhood was spent alone and I was alright with that. I've been social enough when I find myself in social groups, but I've never been one to seek out society. Living on Northwood with The Boys, there was no avoiding it.

Wayne and I were playing one-handed horse shoes at the side of the house on Saturday, our other hands occupied with beer. I was losing, but enjoying the game. Honestly, I would need two hours practice every day for a month to be competitive with Wayne. He was a gracious winner and tried to help me with my technique, without saying much. There was a pretty sizable chunk of tobacco in there, handicapping speech.

Arthur sat on the porch sofa, sipping coffee and reading the newspaper. There was a fly-swatter in his lap. May, Wayne's girlfriend, who was already a student in the vet school, sat on the steps with a magazine. It was a beautiful summer afternoon.

Sid wandered across the street to see if he could play the winner. "Next victim," I joked. Sid's upstairs neighbor, Karl, seeing people enjoying the day out his window, came down and joined Art, with a coffee mug in hand.

After a while, Carly and Mary, both several years older than myself, came walking up the street and stopped to chat. I had yet to meet these two, but Carly looked awfully familiar and I said I thought we'd met before.

"I don't know," she said, "Maybe. I live up near the corner. You've probably seen me around."

Coach whispered to me that *we've met before'* was not the best pick-up line. "No, really," I said. "I think I have."

While we were visiting, Carly did some amazing stretching on the grass. She noticed my watching her. "Yoga saved my life a while back," she said shyly, "after a bad accident."

"I'm into Yoga," I said, "But my body doesn't begin to bend like yours."

Someone mentioned food and a dinner discussion followed. The boys had something for the grill. Mary said she had a dozen ears of corn. There was a watermelon in Karl's fridge. I offered to throw a salad together and Sid volunteered to make a beverage and chips run. As a newcomer, I was surprised how quickly this picnic concept gained momentum.

We all got busy for a while, putting food together. Wayne set the stereo speakers on the porch for a little music. Someone put out lawn chairs and card tables. When the grill was lit, the gathering evolved further, with some friends of friends and another neighbor showing up, most of them bringing contributions to the feast.

After eating, some folks lingered into the evening, talking, sharing, planning, and dancing on the sidewalk. Sid played his guitar for a while and sang a couple of mellow songs he wrote recently. Eventually, the party thinned out, with a few staying to help The Boys clean up. I felt a little overwhelmed by the spontaneity of the event and the pleasure everyone got from it. When I finally rolled into bed, my head was shaking from it all. Art stuck his head in my open door on the way to his room. "Good night," he said, "Welcome to Northwood."

Throwing Darts

In winter or on rainy summer days, the dart board replaced the horseshoe pit as the hub of social interaction at The Boys house. I'm fairly incompetent at darts, too, but love to play. One afternoon, Wayne was thrashing me at a game of Cricket, when Sid and his brother, Dan, came in. When my defeat was complete, I surrendered my darts to Sid and retired on the sofa to visit with Dan. His wife, Lulu, and *soon to be ex*, were best of friends. The staccato sound of darts provided exclamation points to our conversation: thump, thump, thump. I asked how the Hudson Street soap opera was unfolding. *Love is a many splintered thing.*

Dan wanted me to know how difficult our separation was on my wife. He was very serious, describing her sense of loss and loneliness. I told him about seeing her with a guy at Marie's just a few days after we parted, and he affirmed she was seeing other men. What she wanted, according to him, was for me to come back and be okay with that.

"We've evolved into a much more open society," he said. "We can't continue to be tied to the mores of the past!"

"Human nature has not changed," I said.

Dan started to say something else, but Sid turned away from his game to interrupt. "I'm agreeing with Rick, here," he said.

"Me, too," Wayne chimed in.

"Does Lulu make play-dates with other men?" I asked. She mildly hit on me once, but I never mentioned it to Dan.

"Yes, she does," he said, "And I'm okay with it."

Sid couldn't stay out of it. "My brother, I'm so sorry," he said, "But your wife is looking for a replacement. You hurt inside and don't even know it." He returned to his darts. "Don't *ever* get married," he said to Wayne.

I commented about how different these two brothers were, and thankfully, we moved in another direction. Sid and Dan's father was a Methodist minister, and they grew up in the center of a church community, where they were expected to set good examples.

I thought of Sid as an unbeliever, but on Sunday mornings, he could be found singing his favorite hymns, accompanying himself on the guitar. He referred to a *higher power* often, but it sounded more like an anecdotal figure of speech, to me. Religiosity and the reasons people turn to faith was the proposed subject of his dissertation. All that suddenly made sense, hearing about his family life.

Dan, the younger one, took his childhood role seriously, and tried his best to mind his behavior. Sid, in contrast, spent his youth getting into trouble, rebelling against his circumstances.

"He was the classic example of the *bad-boy* preacher's son," Dan said, laughing.

"What do you mean *was*?" Wayne asked. "He still is!"

Crazy Horse

When I got out of my after-work shower on Friday, Sid was in my room sprawled across the bed going through a stack of my photos. "Hey, Coach," I greeted, towel around my waist.

"Oh, Man!" he groaned, "Can I tear this one up?" It was a candid image of himself, with eyes half-mast in dreamy gaze, talking to a young lass on the sidewalk out front.

"Down the memory hole," I said, holding up the waste basket with my free hand. Sid shook his head and ripped it to pieces.

"Now can I get dressed in private?" He turned his back to me on the bed.

"I was thinking about going out and hoisting a few," he said, "Some guys I know are playing at a place in the burbs."

"Let me check my social schedule," I said, pulling on my best jeans. I walked over to Max's calendar and lifted a few pages. "Yes, it appears I'm free for the next several months."

"Ha!" he laughed, "Maybe we can fix that. I heard this was a great venue for meeting girls: desperate, available girls." He smiled devilishly.

I was pretty sure those were not the girls I was looking for, but I could hoist a few. I put on a light summer sports coat to look a bit spiffier, like Coach.

"Don't wait up for me, Honey," I joked with Arthur downstairs as we went out the door. There was still light in the evening sky as Sid and I got into his sporty little car and drove north. "I have got to get some transportation," I lamented. "Left the car with she who has the *full* social schedule."

Sid told me the joint we headed for was called the 'Crazy Horse Saloon'. "Never been there," he said. His friends had a country band: banjo, fiddle, etc. "Not my favorite kind of music, but they're good guys and they can play."

Five or six miles north, we found it, but finding a parking place proved difficult, obviously a popular spot. Inside it was very nice, indeed: clean and tidy around the bar area, with a row of dartboards nearby. We heard the music from a much larger space that opened up away from the bar.

As we walked that way with drinks, a young, well-endowed damsel squeezed by me, though it wasn't that tight a space. As she slid passed, she sort of shoved her breasts against me, which were trying to pop out of her partly unbuttoned blouse. Get the picture? "Excuse me," she gushed breathlessly, with a wink and a smile.

"Wow!" said my coach, "She wants you!"

That was surely not the one I was looking for, if, in fact, I was looking, but stimulating just the same. "Yes," I said, "I really, *really* need an automobile."

The big room had tables around the perimeter, with an area for dancing in the middle. We found an open table near where the band was playing on a low stage in one corner. The suburban nightclub was full of beautiful young people, dressed in style, but uptight somehow. Not that campus area bistros were dirty or ugly, or that their clientele were unkempt, just more relaxed, somehow.

We sipped our drinks, watching people and the band. It was true, they were good musicians in sync with each other. Then I recognized the guitarist. He was the dude having breakfast with my wife at Marie's! My heart pounded out the rhythm for a long minute. Memory is reliving. I told Sid.

"I'm so sorry, man," he said, putting his therapeutic hand on my shoulder, "He's a sweet guy, if you want to meet him. You know, Rick, he might not have been aware she was married at that moment."

I conceded the point, but didn't want to meet him. One drink led to another. I was not the one who was driving, and maybe it was not the best idea to have a car at that particular juncture of my life. Later I threw a game of darts with a stranger, while Sid practiced his craft with a beauty at the bar, coming away with her number. I don't remember a whole lot after that. Sid could probably see I was finished. We drove back to Northwood well before midnight, where I fell into bed, down for the count.

Occupation

My friendly neighborhood on Northwood was a nurturing refuge while recuperating from love lost. Maybe asylum is a better word, since I felt like I was teetering on the razors' edge of sanity much of the time. The sign shop was also a comforting spot to reacquaint myself with living as a single young man, not because my co-workers were all warm and sympathetic, but because the work totally engaged me; the idle mind, etc.

My favorite place there was the darkroom. When I closed the door and turned on the red *safe* light, a yellow light on the other side of the door turned on, warning everyone not to open it for fear of letting in light and spoiling film being developed. If I got bummed out about something, I could duck in there, turn the safe light on, and sort out my thoughts undisturbed. Everyone needs a place with a safe light.

It was a very long room to accommodate the copy camera, which was on train-like tracks, facing a copy board lit up by rows of very bright flood lights on either side. The back of the camera could take a sheet of film up to three feet square. I could pin a logo matchbook on the board, roll the camera to the other end of the room, stretch out the bellows to focus, and make a three foot square photo of the logo on graphic art film. Then I could use that to burn a stencil on a silk-screen and print large signs that look like the matchbook. There is no use for such a camera in the digital age, but, back then, it was an essential tool. I loved the thing.

I made portraits of a couple co-workers and even a selfie with the copy camera. To do this the subject had to be perfectly still for ten seconds. The results were beautiful and unique. Some ways of making art have been lost in the computer world.

When I first started working there, a lot of the art technique and process was alien to me. I was very grateful that my boss, Ray, hired me, and wanted to do good work to show him that was a wise decision. I felt intimidated with so much to learn and started looking around for some help. The guy who seemed to know the most about the tools of the trade and how to use them was Mark, who was deaf.

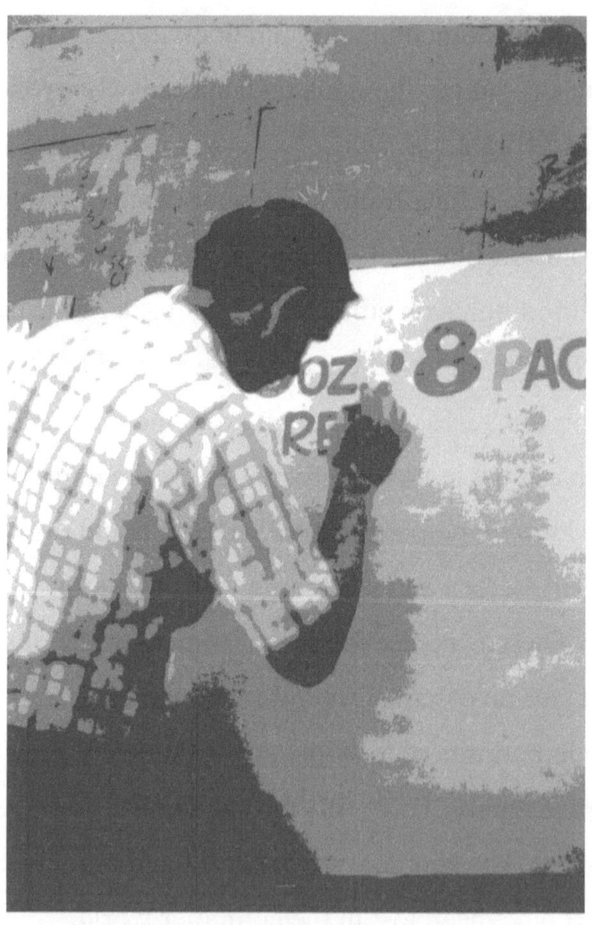

Mark made some pretty strange sounds when he tried to talk, making it very difficult for anyone there to communicate with him. When The Brothers were around, they sometimes made fun of him behind his back. Mostly people left him alone to work by himself and he looked content to do that.

After my first few days there, I went to the student book store by campus and found an instructional manual for learning deaf sign language and finger spelling. I poured over it for a few days before getting up the courage to try some signing with him. Then one morning, I got Marks' attention and signed, "It's time for break. Ten o'clock."

He looked at me blankly for a moment and then busted out laughing. He dipped his lettering brush in paint thinner and wiped it off with a cloth, shaking his head, while I wondered what the hell was so damn funny. At break, he sat by me and carefully showed me the *correct* way to form the signs with my hands. I was learning from drawings, not video, and signing clumsily. Later in the day he showed me a few more useful signs I hadn't seen in the book, yet.

Mark appreciated my desire to learn his lingo and helped me with the process. He also began teaching me all about the sign business. Most importantly, he became my friend. After a few months, we could converse fairly smoothly about our lives, politics, the weather, and gossip.

A problem for the deaf is that people over-enunciate their words and emphasize their mouth movement, thinking it will help them read the lips. The opposite is true. Mark could lip-read casual conversation from across the room. He knew what people were saying quietly to each other, what Ray said when talking to customers, and what everyone said on the phone. This man had the dirt on everybody and was none too shy about sharing some of it with me as we became friendly. In turn, I shared what I heard from behind backs with him.

Our ease of parlance generated some negative vibes around the place. Our boss, Ray, and the other sign painters had worked with Mark for years, struggling to connect with him. Now, this kid shows up and, in a couple months, is talking and laughing with him over lunch. But when someone couldn't get the details of a project across to him, they sometimes asked me to interpret. Ray could see I was learning sign painting technique from Mark, and frequently gave me a "good job" when I finished something difficult. Gradually the situation was accepted and normalcy returned. The thing is, I cared enough to learn Mark's language. Sometimes I'm more *carpe diem* than *go with the flow*.

Mental Health

Dubbing Mary 'McFreud' when I first met her must have been some kind of inspired, or maybe just hopeful, premonition. She was so very good at drawing stuff out of me I didn't know was there. But she cleverly made me do all the work, coaxing me closer and closer to the precipice I was terrified to look over. It was frightening, but exhilarating, and I began looking forward to our sessions.

One afternoon, I was way early for my appointment and sat outside on a bench by the sidewalk. A young guy came up and asked directions, but silently, with pencil and notebook. I signed, "Are you deaf?" He heaved a sigh and sat down with me. Very cool, I thought, here's my chance to see if I can use what I've learned. Then he started talking too fast with his hands. "Go slow," I signed, "I'm still learning." Then we connected, had a little chat, and I drew a map in his notebook to show him where he wanted to go.

My time with Mary began with her asking me if I was getting out and meeting people. "Other than in bars," she said.

"Well, yeah," I talked about meeting a lot of people when I first got to Northwood but, now that I'm settled in, I felt more isolated, which was alright with me.

"Are you in Mensa?" she asked. "They have a lot of social activities."

"Mensa?" I asked, "You think I'm Mensa material? If I'm one of the smart ones, this world is in a lot of trouble. I doubt if smart people have as many problems as I do."

"Smart people especially have problems like you," she said, "because they think about and analyze everything. They're not sleep-walking through life." She asked why I didn't think I was very smart.

"I don't know," I said, "I had a few teachers who seemed very disappointed in me."

"I saw you out my window talking with that deaf man," she said, "Where did you pick that up?"

"There's a deaf guy at work I want to get to know," I said. I told her about Mark and my book of signs and finger-spelling.

"And you've been working on that for how long?" she asked.

"A couple months, I guess," I said.

"So you've learned the basics of deaf sign language and finger-spelling in a couple months, but you're not smart." she said, frowning.

Then I heard that voice in my head, the voice that called me stupid every day. My older brother who thought I was his personal punching bag. "*Stupid* kid!" I mimicked my brother to Mary. "Everything you do is so *stupid*!" I began to feel my guts tighten and became agitated as I told Mary about my childhood. "What a *stupid* thing to say! How could you be so *stupid*?"

"But you love him," Mary stated quietly.

"God damn it! He's my brother!" I said, as if that were an answer. "My arms were black and blue all the time. Sometimes he'd grab my wrist and hit me with my own hand. I was helpless to stop him. He cheated me out of my paper route money. He went into my room and destroyed my most precious things, just to be a jerk. We're adults and he's still a jerk to me! And he still calls me *stupid* and belittles everything I do and say!"

With very few words, Mary skillfully led me to this place where I was seething with anger. Then she casually pulled an empty chair over to us. "Don't tell me," she said, "Tell him." She pointed to the chair.

"Oh, come on, Mary," I said, shaking my head, "That's just an empty chair." I smiled, thinking it was a pretty silly game to play.

"Yes," she said with all seriousness, "The chair is empty and he's not really here, so you won't hurt his feelings." She put her hand on my arm and met my eyes. "And he can't hurt you." She pointed to the chair more firmly. "Tell him!"

The volcano erupted. Bursting into tears I shouted, "You son of a bitch!" I jumped up shouting with fists clenched, "You ruined my life!" My entire body was in a knot. I kicked over the chair and fell back down, heaving deep sobs.

Mary, still perfectly calm, handed me her box of tissues. She probably goes through a lot of those. "That's good," she said, nodding, "Catharsis is good progress. I didn't think you'd have an *event* so soon."

Calmness fell over me as I wiped my eyes. It was a calm I hadn't experienced for a long time. "Damn!" I exclaimed, "That felt great!"

"Let's start on some epiphanies next time," she said with a comforting smile, "Those can be a little trickier."

I laughed, dabbing my eyes with tissues. "Yeah!" I said, "I like the sound of that!"

Dick's Den

There is no shortage of taverns in Columbus, Ohio, but each one has its own unique charm, or lack thereof. My personal sorrow drowning sanctuary of choice was Dick's Den on North High, which drew a somewhat educated, young adult demographic. It also had the advantage of being in reasonable walking distance of Northwood, if stranded or incapacitated.

The Dick's Den Marathon, every Saint Patrick's Day, was a well-known event in the north Columbus area. I guess it could be called a biathlon, involving both drinking and running from Dick's to a liquor store to the north, buying a bottle of Jameson, then running back with it. I never participated, but observed the contest a couple times, green beer in hand.

At that time my athleticism did not go beyond the pool table. There was a comfortable little back room with one at Dick's, which I gravitated to whenever I was there. As a regular, I got to know some of the characters who shared my love of the game. There was a community atmosphere around the table, not as warm and nurturing as my Northwood neighborhood, but agreeable in its way, making the place a disarming haven. Molly, a taxi driver and frequent player, could probably arm wrestle anyone in the place and win. John, an exception to the youthful crowd, was an old retired cop, who told grizzly *dragnet* stories while he played. He smoked a cigar, so you could tell he was there as soon as you entered the bar.

Then there was Mack, who was almost always there, as if he lived there. After knowing him only a short while, I could see he was a loser. Mack was like a professional loser, with maybe a degree from the Ohio institute of losing. If losing were an Olympic event, Mack would take the gold. He was terrible with a cue stick, because he couldn't see. The lenses in his glasses were so thick, it made his eyes look large and owl like.

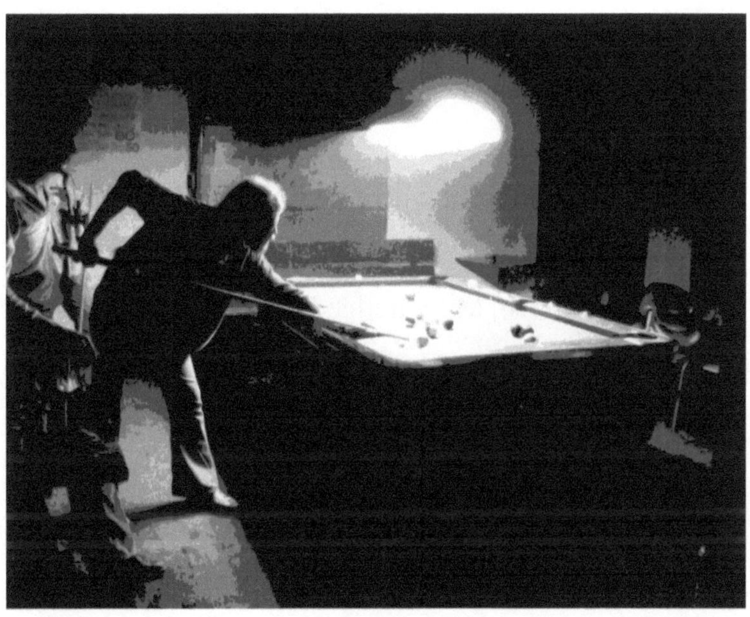

Mack invariably wanted to bet a drink on a game, but always lost. When he wasn't playing, he sat looking sadly at the floor, occasionally letting out a quiet 'God dammit' and slamming his fist down on his knee. I found myself giving him a friendly pat on the back when I saw his anguish, but didn't think we'd become friends. Then one morning at work, I walked out of my darkroom and saw that Ray hired Mack! "You're a sign painter?" I asked, totally surprised, "With *your* eyes?"

"I can see," he said, defending himself. "This is my third sign shop. I've been doing this for seven or eight years." When I watched him working later, he looked like he knew what he was doing with a lettering brush.

"You know him?" Mark asked in sign.

"I met him at a bar I go to," I signed.

Mark, a non-drinking family man, asked, "Is he a drunk?"

"Not really, I signed, "but he's a very sad person. I don't know why."

Mack looked up from where he was cleaning a brush. "Are you guys talking about me?" he asked.

Later, after lunch, Mark nudged me and pointed to Mack, standing at the far end of the long lettering easel, with his head leaning against it.

"I see what you mean," Mark signed, "He's swearing."

Working together, I got to know Mack better and started hanging out with him after work sometimes. Maybe I identified with him. Did being around such a hapless sad-sack make me feel better about myself? Or did I just want more friends with cars?

Mom & Dad

It's a blessing to have loving, supportive parents. Mine helped me in many ways throughout life. The only real complaint I have with them is that they didn't, or maybe couldn't, stop my brother from abusing me. There was a drive to the emergency room to have a cut in my head stitched up. Running away from my brother with all I had, I slipped and hit my forehead on the corner of a table. "You boys play too roughly!" my mother said in the car.

"I'm not playing!" I cried. They didn't understand what was going on.

With so many traumas and changes that first summer on Northwood, I thought a weekend back home in the loving arms of Mom & Dad would give me a boost. Simply seeing a couple get along after living together for decades would be a pleasure.

The thought came to me as I walked home from work on a Friday night. As soon as I got to my room at The Boy's house, I grabbed my dirty clothes duffle, said some goodbyes, and left to hitch-hike two hundred miles home. It's a miracle I got there.

These were the problems: I walked to the freeway in flip-flops and didn't even *bring* shoes. There were only about ten bucks in my wallet. It was warm, at the moment, so I didn't bring a jacket or even a hat. I didn't call ahead to let Mom & Dad know I was coming.

For several youthful years, I was a Boy Scout: a leader in my troop, taught pioneering merit badge at scout camp, and hiked in the wilderness often. But that weekend, *be prepared* was not on my agenda. It really shows how thinking straight abandons you when your life is a mess. Or maybe it's the other way around.

At I-71, a sixteen wheeler picked me up almost right away. The trucker and I visited for a while, but I was so tired, and damn! I'm going home! I fell dead asleep in his truck.

He shook my arm to waken me when his exit came and wished me well as I climbed down to the road on a two lane bridge. But he didn't tell me where we were. I looked up and down the crossroads and didn't see I-71! The sky was dark and thunder sounded. One road was nameless and the other was state route twenty-one, which meant nothing to me. But the ramp on the other side of the bridge said *north* 21 and north sounded good.

As I walked across, rain began. Hitch-hiking *under* the bridge seemed like the best idea, so I climbed over the guard rail in a big hurry as soon as I got to the other side. But my pant leg caught on a jagged edge of metal, tearing the cloth and my flesh. I fell, rolling down the embankment, losing one of my flip-flops. Limping with one bare foot, I got under the bridge and out of the rain which was now a downpour.

It was that moment, bleeding on rocks under a highway bridge, in a thunderstorm, and lost, that I realized what I dolt I was. I got a sick feeling in my guts, thinking about how all this could have been avoided. And then something unexpected happened. I started reciting the Boy Scout oath. "On my honor, I will do my best to do my duty," I said out loud, assessing my situation. "To help other people at all times," I continued. I took a sock out of my laundry bag, cut the toe off with my pocket knife, and pulled it over my leg to protect my wound. "To keep myself physically strong, mentally awake, and morally straight," I finished, moving on to the scout laws.

As the rain continued and the temperature dropped, I pulled a couple long sleeve layers from my laundry and put them on. Night was falling and I did my best to make a soft, dry place under the bridge to sleep. And I did sleep. It was probably the best possible sleep a lost, injured person could have under a strange bridge in a cold rain. Just saying.

In the morning, I tried without luck to find my other flip-flop. There were a couple of dark socks in my bag I put on to *look* like shoes for hitch-hiking. When I put out my thumb, my sock feet were hidden behind my duffle. Providence served me again and a salesman stopped to pick me up. I held my feet to the side, hoping he would not see that I had no shoes. "Where the heck am I?" I asked with a smile, explaining my nap in the earlier truck ride.

My savior told me we were going in the right direction and his path took us right past my desired exit. When we got there, he volunteered to get off and drop me at my childhood home. Maybe he was a Boy Scout, too.

I thanked him as strongly as I could and wearily walked up the familiar driveway. There was the swing in the old oak tree, the garage I helped Dad build several years ago, and the vegetable garden in its late summer glory. But all was quiet. Their old car was there, but Mom and Dad were not home.

I found the ladder in the garage and climbed on the roof to my old bedroom window. This was teenage late night déjà vu. Once inside, I washed my clothes and myself, nursed the cut on my leg, and had a relaxing couple days. Not everything was familiar at the house. Mom and Dad started a little gift shop as a fun retirement project, which started with a lot of local hand-crafted items. Then they made a couple print bins and filled them with New York Graphic Society prints. The latest I heard was that Dad took a class in picture framing. Now there were framed prints on the walls and a nicely equipped framing workshop in the basement. It was the same comforting old homestead, but way different, too.

I thought my folks might be back and decided to call off work Monday morning, long distance. Sunday evening, they arrived home in their new car. "Bought it last week," Dad said, "and thought we'd take it for a little jaunt." Then they dropped the bomb. "We weren't offered much in trade for our old one," he said, "so we thought you might like to have it."

"Oh my God!" I hugged them both together and gushed my appreciation. It was a spotless 1965 Buick Skylark with only a hundred thousand miles on it. I was no longer a pedestrian.

The next evening, I sat in a corner of Karl's darkroom, relating my weekend saga while he worked. The prints emerging in his developing tray were thoughtful people photos depicting lives in

crisis. He empathized with my story and told me some of his own.
A couple weeks later these pictures were displayed at a facility that
fed the homeless. He titled the exhibit: *I Too Have Slept Under
Bridges.* Thanks Karl.

The Loft

Several doors up and across the street from The Boys was an
old house surrounded by some equally old, encroaching Hemlocks.
Both house and yard needed loving care, but there was a friendly,
inviting quality that drew my attention.

The apartment downstairs was occupied by a mysterious,
quiet young man who wore prescription sun glasses night and day,
difficult to look into his eyes. He was a tall, slender guy I noticed
coming and going, but kept to himself and didn't participate in social
activity on the street. In contrast, the very young lady living upstairs
was a flagrant extrovert. She showed up at a minor Friday evening
beer fest in The Boy's yard, shortly after I moved in. It was flip-flop
weather, but she wore high boots with colorful knee socks rising out
of them. I called her Pippi Longstocking, which fit her like a glove.
She playfully stuck her tongue out and told me she was Suzie. Then
she went up on the porch and energetically danced with the music,
beer in hand.

Sid came over and suggested Suzie was the one to jump-start
my sex life. "Play your guitar for her and she'll jump right into your

bed," he said. "She's a rock and roll sycophant, a local band groupie." Just then, she started a crazy laugh that sounded more like a scream. No thanks, Coach.

Several weeks later, I heard a rumor that she was vacating her apartment. Art and Wayne were great, but I longed for my own place and Max would want his room back in September. I immediately walked over and knocked on Suzie's door to see if it was true. She needed to get out of her lease and I was overjoyed to assume it. I was delirious to know I would stay in my new-found Northwood refuge. A week later, she moved out and I moved in.

Suzie, no kidding, painted the living room ceiling black, but I decided to leave it that way, at first. I thought I might get out my paints and turn it into a starry night with familiar constellations. It didn't make the room look dark, because large windows on three sides filled the place with light and air. Standing in the middle of it, looking up, down, and across the street, I called my new place 'The Loft'.

The kitchen was small, but adequate. Suzie left half a pizza hidden in the broiler, which ignited the first time I lit the oven. I walked into the living room, but quickly returned when billowing dark smoke poured out of the kitchen door and windows. Concerned neighbors ran up my stairs to see if the place was on fire and found me hosing down a charcoal pizza in the sink.

The bedroom was large enough to double as my darkroom, without feeling cramped. I did my photo printing late at night, so I wouldn't have to block light from the windows. Seeing the red glow of my safe light and the repeated on and off of my white light had people wondering about me at first.

After moving my stuff in, which wasn't much, I plopped on the sofa with my guitar, stretching my feet out on my footlocker, which was going to serve as a coffee table. To me, home was wherever my guitar and trunk were. I began picking a twangy Mississippi John Hurt tune about relationship gone sour, the theme I was wallowing in.

Suddenly, not so quiet mystery man below startled me, bounding up the stairs with his guitar. "You know Mississippi!" he exclaimed! We played the song together, before introducing ourselves. He was Les, a musician and commercial arts student, among other things.

"I work in graphic arts at a sign company," I said.

He laughed. "Wow," he said, "You're a breath of fresh air after 'Boots'." His name for Suzie was not a term of endearment. "She played nothing but Aerosmith on her stereo!" he lamented, "I thought I was going to lose my mind!"

Dream

I dreamed that I became deaf, but was joyful, because I knew sign language, thinking it wasn't much of a handicap. I was in front of my easel working on a painting and thinking about how wonderful it was not to be blind. Painting along happily, I thought it might be about to rain. I turned to look out the window and saw that it was already raining quite steadily. Suddenly, I was sick at heart, because I would never hear the sound of the rain again. Waking up, I found it was, in fact, raining with distant thunder and lightning. For a long time I lay awake in bed, listening.

Dreaming

Living alone means farting freely. Turning on a light by the bed at two in the morning to read a bit will not disturb anyone. There are no negotiations about what to cook for dinner. The bathroom is always free when you need it. There are also some drawbacks, but I couldn't think of any.

Dreaming is a life-long interest of mine, and I struggle to remember and write down the details when I have a good one. I was aware that if the head is kept in the dreaming position after waking, recall is easier. But who can write in that position? I set up my tape recorder next to the bed with the microphone in easy reach, and started verbally recording dream description, without moving my head. There was no one whose sleep I might disturb by talking out loud. Morning light quickly erased remembrance of the night, but in the evening after work, I'd listen to my long recordings and be amazed. Hearing myself talk brought recollection of the dream back with clarity I hadn't experienced before. Talking to myself became a *good* thing.

This exercise taught me volumes about the dream state and more. In waking life, we have various organs that sense our environment. Then the brain interprets that sensory information and *creates* our perception of the world around us. In dreaming, the opposite is happening. The brain gives us the *perception* of vision, but our eyes are closed.

The first thing I noticed in my recorded late night babbling was that I used words to describe things that, in waking, I reserve for other things. For example, I often use the words flexible and rigid to describe states of being. Yet, I heard myself calling a brick wall rigid, as if a brick wall could be anything else. Mulling that over, I realized the wall in my dream was a *symbol* for a state of being and a very different way to talk to myself.

One night I woke from a dream in which a very profound thought about relationships came to me. I reached for the microphone without moving my head, and excitedly jabbered away about it. When I listened to my voice later, there was no mention of epiphanies! I described my ex, my brother, Mom & Dad, and myself, all living in glass rooms: separate, but in plain sight of each other. Disappointed at first, but then I saw that the images *were* the profound thought! In the dream I understood it with clarity on some level, but didn't get it when I woke up.

People talked to me in dreams, but then I saw that they didn't. There was some other communication of images that I perceived as a voice. In dreaming, I not only put thoughts into images, but sounds too. It was very difficult and, I'm sure, inaccurate, to articulate into the microphone words I only *thought* I was hearing.

Seeing that sensation, reality, and perception do not equate in dreams, made me question the same in waking life. The mundane parable is the police officer who gets four eye-witness accounts of an accident and they're all very different. But it's not just that we don't agree on reality, it's that *none* of us, in fact, *knows* reality.

None of this was helping me negotiate the quagmire of everyday living, so I tried to refocus my efforts back to understanding what I might be telling myself with dreams, instead of trying to figure out what the hell dreams are.

Then one night Lynne, my high school classmate, came to me in a dream. That's all I remembered through the day, but knew I used the tape recorder and looked forward to getting the whole picture. I thought it might be one that spoke to my life's progress. That night I listened and it all came back.

I was driving along a particular street in my home town near Cleveland. There was something wrong with the car, which was full of empty boxes, and I was worried. Then I was at a gas station at the corner of the street and saw Lynne working there. She was dressed in dirty coveralls and had grease smudges on her face. I wanted to ask her something about happiness, but she was busy looking my car over. She indicated that I needed an oil change and, in two seconds, had the job done. I got back in the car, intending to go home, but was somehow lost, even though I knew where I was. I was in the car, trying to decide which way to turn, when I awoke. I turned off the tape and puzzled over the dream. What were all these symbols to me: the car, empty boxes, Lynne, and oil changing? Which way should I turn?

Stop Me, Please

My dream recording project launched me into deep thinking on a number of subjects related to perception and reality. It distracted me at work. The red *safe light* in the darkroom made the red of the fire extinguisher on the wall look gray. Pink things looked white, too. We rely on our senses to experience our world, but the darkroom played tricks on my eyes. Maybe there is some kind of cosmic *safe light* that hides certain elements of the *real* world from us.

Time bothered me. The future is always the future. You could say it arrives, but then it's the present. It seemed to me that the only time that really exists is the present moment. P. D. Ouspensky, the Russian philosopher, wrote that time was a misperceived dimension in space. Maybe he was crazier than I am.

The present moment might also be a glimpse at infinity, since a moment has no duration. Just like a line in mathematics has an infinite number of points, there are an infinite number of moments in a minute. If, like in a dream, you could turn that thought into a sensation, what would it be?

Lucky Penny

It occurred to me that time was the common element to all energy producing processes. From lighting a candle to nuclear fusion, time must elapse. Could all energy producing processes be indirectly harnessing the power of time itself?

Time passing is also the essential element for experiencing love, life, death, joy, and pain. Does *being here now* alter our perception of those? Ideas started causing me anxiety.

To stop thinking crazy thoughts at work, I put a small radio in my work area and sang along with the music: silk screen karaoke.

After work on Friday night, I wanted to join the ritual of millions around the world and pour myself a liquid lobotomy. At Dick's I wandered through the crowd of regulars and found Mack sitting by the pool table, looking depressed. We played a few games of eight-ball. I wondered out loud if games, especially games of chance, were incumbent on our perception of time.

Mack, who had been hearing some of my wonderings all week at work, begged me to give it a break. "Stop thinking!" he said. "If, as you say, the moment is all that exists, just be here now and enjoy it." He shook his head as he lined up the next shot. "Listen to me," he said, "I'm starting to sound like you."

After Dick's we went for a sandwich at the Blue Danube, epitome of the American diner. Time definitely stands still there. The place hasn't changed in decades. The food was tolerable and we visited with some friends. I relaxed and lapsed into the comfort of small talk. When we left the 'Dube', I was ready to go home and offered Mack a lift to his place. He said he thought he'd walk, but leaned on the open passenger window talking with me for a long time. "Get in," I repeated, "I'll drive you home."

"Alright," he said, climbing in, "I guess I'd rather ride, than take a hike."

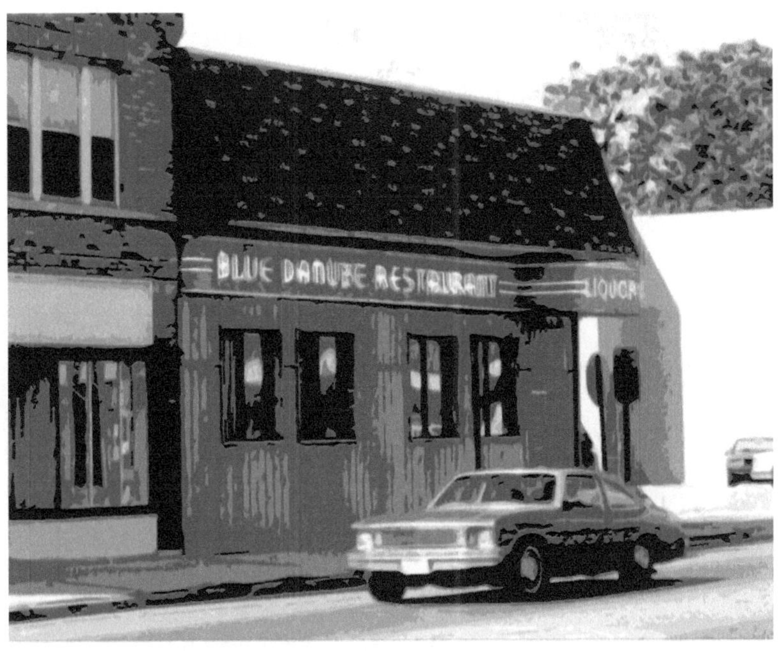

High Street is all downhill from the diner to campus, and I idled out from the curb, not in any kind of hurry. We rolled down slowly to the first stop light. I stepped on the brake pedal, which caught briefly, then slipped to the floor without resistance! My heart exploded in my chest!

"That was a red light, Mister," Mack drawled comically with his John Wayne impression.

"No brakes!" I shouted!

"What!?" Mack gasped, sitting up, "Emergency!"

"Tried that!" I said, "Not there!"

"Low gear!" Mack strapped on his seatbelt.

"Yeah, low gear!" I said, shifting, "That helps, good." We were moving very slowly, but downhill is downhill.

"Dear God, save us!" Mack prayed. "They'll be a ton of people crossing at Lane. Pray for a green light! We can't hurt anyone, I couldn't bear it."

"Streets left go up," I said, "Help me see one open."

"That one!" Mack pointed, "Maynard!"

"It's one way down!" I said, "Next one!

"Turn off the key!" Mack ordered!

"Yeah!" I said, and then, "No! Gonna need power steering!" We were approaching twenty miles-per-hour.

"People crossing Patterson!" Mack shouted, "Damn! Plow into a pole if you have to, but stop this thing before Lane!"

"A sign post might do it," I said, trying to think. "Northwood coming up!"

"It's clear!" Mack shouted, putting both hands out to hold the dashboard, "Do it!"

I went as far right as I could, for a rounded *farmer* turn. The tires screeched and we felt the force, but we made it. Going uphill, we slowed to a crawl. I inched up to the first long open parking spot, pulled to the curb, and threw it into park. Northwood saved me again.

We were both in a state of shock as we sat back breathing deeply. "That *could* have gone very badly," I sighed. We slowly got out and found our land legs on the sidewalk.

"Tell Ray I'll be late to work Monday," I said, imagining the logistics of a tow truck to the service station. We began walking up Northwood.

"Next time," Mack said, "I'm walking home."

Maximum Max

Max returned from the Pacific Northwest with stories to tell. His job, can you believe, was to wander a large section of the Olympic wilderness, identifying and counting wildlife species. Apparently, he ate quite a few, as well. Terrific storms, survival issues, and bear encounters, Max had quite a summer.

He related the experience of running out of food far from his resupply location and feeling desperate. He came upon a small injured deer, roped it, and proceeded to stone it to death, feeling ashamed. The wilderness momentarily reverted him into primitive man. Hunger: emotional, sexual, intellectual, and creative, are all forces that can drive people to act crazily. Is someone out there truly satisfied, or are we all hungry to some extent?

A little welcome home gathering for Max in the bosom of the neighborhood was in order. It looked like we might get some version of rain, so I helped Max put up a couple tarps over tables out front. At a corner I tied a quick bowline through the grommet and a taught-line hitch around the porch railing.

"You were a Boy Scout," Max observed

"I *am* a Boy Scout, brother," I said, thinking he and I might connect after all. "Somewhere on my path, I lapsed for a while, but I'm back on track, now."

"Life is a test," Max said, "We all have a few scars."

The wild look in his eyes made me think he had more than a few. Sid found Max an interesting study and asked if he wouldn't mind taking one of his personality profile tests, claiming he needed subjects for his dissertation research. Max declined to participate.

I didn't know him very well, but Sid told me to look no further to gage my mental health progress. "You are the active experiment," he said, "Max is the control group."

As our little barbecue progressed, I saw that sincerity was the dominant feature of his aura. He warmly greeted everyone. A political discussion arose and his firmly expressed position was adamant and heart-felt, if not well thought out. A pretty young thing, friend of a friend, arrived and Max fell deeply and sincerely in love with her in a moment. Later that month, he fell out of love, just as quickly and just as sincerely, another anti-role model for me.

Open House

Les, my downstairs neighbor, and I got along very well. He was a bright guy from a white-collar middle class family who had interests and a world view similar to my own. We usually had our doors open and often dropped in on each other to visit, have a drink or play music together, and sometimes share a meal. I talked him into joining me a couple times in some neighborhood interaction and he became somewhat acquainted with other characters on Northwood, but remained aloof. We are who we are.

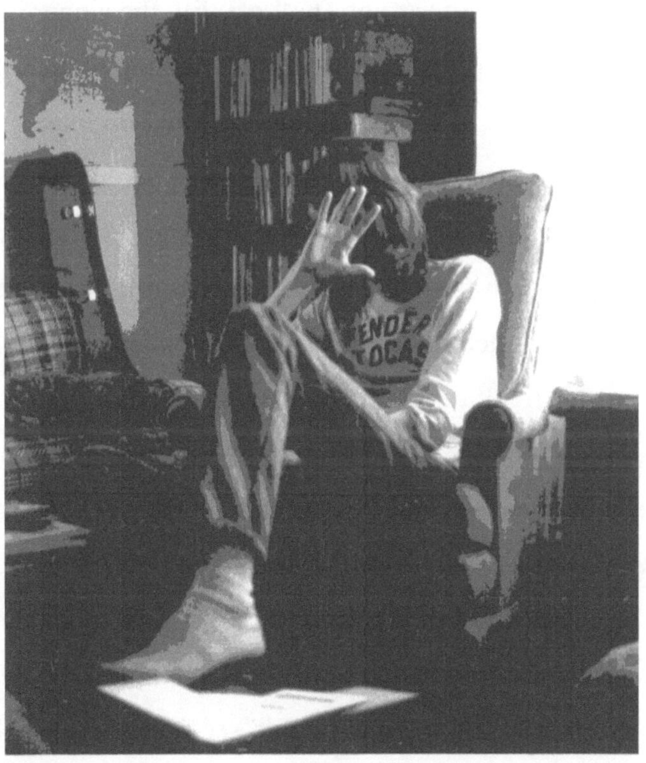

To help pay his bills, Les worked part-time at a music store, gave some guitar lessons, and had a small band that got occasional paying gigs, but never any steady work. He also sold stuff with ads in the classified section of the paper or stapled to campus bulletin boards. Interested buyers stopped by, checked out the items, and paid cash. Then there would be a new collection of nice stuff in his apartment that he'd say he *found* and wanted to flip for a profit. Where does one *find* an eight hundred dollar Moog Synthesizer or a matching set of Persian rugs? If I asked, he would deftly change the subject which was fine with me, because I really didn't want to know. It wasn't drugs or guns he was selling.

A few months after I got The Loft, Jill, the singer in the band, split up with her husband, who was cheating on her. She moved in with Les for a while, having few other options. Devastated by the turn of her life, she often came up to The Loft, seeing in me a sympathetic listener who had recently been traveling the same road. She was smart, witty, and beautiful, but I enjoyed our friendship and tried not think about her romantically. Her sexuality was difficult to ignore, but I wasn't ready.

Jill soon found a place of her own, but spent most weekends at our house because she and Les became lovers. The downstairs apartment was larger than mine and Les liked it rather dark, keeping the curtains closed most of the time. Jill, who was quite slender like Les, also wore prescription sun glasses all the time. The two of them favored black clothing and I could see something of Gomez and Morticia Addams in them. Once in a while they *found* some

Quaaludes and sedated themselves, a popular recreational drug at the time, but one I couldn't understand. Like most of my generation, I smoked my share of pot for its energetic effect, but why would anyone want to be down? But, as I said earlier, we got along great, and The Loft was a comfortable, Bohemian place to live.

One night, Jill wandered up under the influence and lay down on top of me where I reclined on the sofa with a book. "Do you like me?" she asked in a slurred whisper.

"Sure I do," I said, holding her in my arms, "You are very likable, Jill." She kissed me with open mouth. "That's very nice," I told her, "but, honestly, I think I need a friend more than a lover right now."

She brightened and looked me in the eye. "That's what I need!" Slowly she reached up and took my face in her hands. "Friends," she said, and gave me a kiss of an entirely different nature. Then her body went limp and she fell asleep, like turning off a light, snoring softly with her head on my chest.

Love nest, or not

The Loft was a mess for quite a while. Moving means boxes and there was a small stack of them. There were priorities, like setting up the darkroom corner of the bedroom. One of the first things I did was get out my paints and put a blank canvas on my easel in the living room so I could start trying to capture the ambiance of my airy garret overlooking Northwood. I also found myself just lounging around on the sofa with a beer, basking in the blessed solitude of my own space. The boxes could wait.

I was feeling more relaxed, not thinking *every day* about my spouse. We would be signing separation papers soon to legally be free of each other. She got the car, all our furniture, and most of the other material evidence of our union. I got a chunk of our savings, the photo stuff, some tools, and my books. It would take more time to retrieve my sanity. It was time to start a new chapter of my life. I wanted to take advantage of this living alone thing, find out who I really was and map out my soul. All I had to do was avoid any traps that might take me away from that.

Mary and my coach down the street were trying to tell me it was a good idea to get out and meet some single women, but I hadn't had a real yin-yang date in years and didn't want one now. Any prospect coming up here, I thought, would turn right around and leave. It was not *house beautiful.* Basic essentials were missing, like a toaster, TV, and vacuum sweeper. The bedroom was part darkroom, the living room was part art studio, and there were a few rolls of film hanging down from a clothesline in the bathroom to dry. What woman would melt into my arms in this environment?

Then I was proven so completely wrong. Here was an available man and every woman in town who knew him stopped by, many of them strongly intimating that they'd love to have sex with an artsy guy in his shabby eccentric abode. But what you *really*

want comes into better focus when what you *think* you want happens
and you just don't feel that way about any of the gals showing up.

All except the married one, the wife of an old friend. Their
knot was slowly untying after a few rocky years. Getting it on with
someone's wife was definitely cognitive dissonance, but she had
become a good friend, too, and that somehow made the idea of
sleeping with her more attractive. It was an interesting thought I
filed away to chew on later. Without much hesitation, I turned her
away, too.

One of the visiting women brought me a cat, asking if I
wanted a roommate. I tried to glean any innuendo from this gesture,
but decided she simply wanted to give me a cat. The animal was
beautiful and house broken, so I decided to keep her. She prowled
around The Loft, hunting. A game, I thought, but then she came up
with a mouse! After a few days, she warmed up to me and jumped
from the floor to my shoulder when I came home from work. That
was when I named her Bagheera, after the cat in Kipling's *Jungle
Books*.

Independence

Bagheera started meowing the moment my key met the front
door lock. Feeding her became my first priority at the loft after
work. My second was washing the smell of paint off in the shower,

but as I set the cat food dish on the floor, I heard Jill charging up the stairs shouting my name.

"What's wrong!?" I asked, meeting her at the top.

"Nothing's wrong!" she laughed, "I got a job!" She jumped up and down and spun in a circle. "Everything's right!"

"That's great!" I said, returning to the kitchen. "What, where, and when?"

Early that morning, Jill came upstairs to pour over the help-wanted ads in my morning paper. She circled several and started back down carrying the paper without enthusiasm. Now she was bursting with it.

"I applied for a bunch of horrible jobs and passed the Record Outlet on my way home, which is where I really wanted to work," she said. "I'm a regular customer and sort of know everybody. So I walked in and asked if they needed help. I was all nervous, but they hired me!"

There was some ginger ale in the fridge which I poured into long stemmed glasses for pretend champagne, handing her one. I held the other aloft and proposed the toast. "To financial independence," I intoned.

"Ha!" she said, taking a sip. "Financial and every other Goddamn way!"

I heard her words with a part of me deep inside. "Yeah," I said. "To self empowerment." We clinked our glasses again.

"I can't stay long," she said. "It starts tomorrow and I'm not ready."

"Not ready?" I asked.

"Of course not!" she said. "I have to go shopping for new clothes!" She shook her head in disbelief, half-smiling. "Men," she muttered.

Cops

Every weekday morning around ten, an independent coffee-break catering truck came to the complex of buildings the sign shop shared with a few other businesses. One such morning, Ray's brother, a city police officer, was visiting. He was very into his image, with that spit-shine uniform look, which made me a little uncomfortable. He had a good sense of humor, though, and everyone seemed to like him. But that morning, he did a sleazy cop thing that took me by surprise and still twists my guts when I think about it.

The police officer took coffee and doughnuts from the truck without paying, giving the caterer a look as he walked by. I was shocked and asked the guy when I paid for my coffee. He told me city cops routinely did that. I tried to give him an extra buck knowing his income was a fraction of the cop's, but he refused to accept it. *Someone* had integrity.

Instead of sitting with everyone for the usual break time chatter, I went to the darkroom, set my coffee down on the light table, and shook all over with rage. What a lousy, rotten world this is. Mark saw me in there as he walked by and stopped short. He came in and put his hand on my shoulder, the question on his face. All I could do was shake. There is a single deaf language sign which means holding strong emotion inside. He told me not to. I broke into tears, letting it out as I told him what happened. It's wrong, my hands said.

Mark nodded his head at my youthful agitation with a fatherly look in his eyes, agreeing it was wrong. The officer was flawed like all men, he told me, but not a bad guy overall. "Not a complete pig," he signed. I used the word earlier, but finger-spelled it. He taught me the sign for it, repeating it with an exaggerated, comical motion that started to bring my good humor back.

Mark wrote something on a piece of scrap paper and left to join the others. I stayed in the darkroom to compose myself. Besides, I didn't want to see the cop eating his doughnuts. But then I heard a big commotion going on and came out of my safety zone. Mark knew our boss well enough to give him the scrap paper which said, "Your brother did not pay the coffee man."

Ray blew his top and told his brother he was ashamed of him. They argued a while, until the cop left in a huff, saying Ray didn't understand the *unwritten* laws of the city.

The next morning, Ray apologized to the caterer and insisted on paying his brother's debt with a ten dollar bill. "You keep the change!"

Curly

A dead squirrel lay in the middle of Northwood when I got out of my car after work. They almost seem suicidal, the way they dash across the street. I hoped it wasn't the one that frequented the porch roof outside my kitchen window. But while I was eating later, I noticed something move in the pine needles. I opened the window and leaned out for a closer look. It was a tiny hairless baby squirrel whose eyes were yet to open.

I sat back down and pushed my plate away. Suddenly I felt sick to my stomach. That was Mom out on the road, and this little thing with an instinct for survival crawled out of the nest and fell on my roof. As I looked out at it, thinking, another one fell from the hemlock and landed near the first. Should I let nature take its course, or try to help them? Was it even possible to help them? Wayne could probably answer that one.

Bagheera jumped up to the table, and I quickly shut the window. The movement on the roof had her complete attention. She meowed and pawed at the glass. Letting nature take its course was her choice, and she was willing to help out with that. I picked her up and closed her in the bedroom.

I found a shoebox, put a soft rag inside, and climbed out on the porch roof. Now there were three. I carefully picked up their warm, wiggling bodies and placed them the box. After searching the gutter and the tree debris, I thought there would be no others, but waited and watched a while longer to make sure. Then I went down to the The Boys house, feeling low. It looked pretty hopeless to me.

Fortunately, both Wayne and his vet school girlfriend, May, were there. Wayne looked serious and shook his head when he saw them, but May immediately went out to the kitchen and got some milk and an eye-dropper. "There's an infant formula I can get," she said, "but let's try milk for now." One by one, she picked them up and gave them an opportunity to get nourishment. Two of them went at it eagerly, but the third was somewhat lethargic.

I expressed doubt that I could do what she was doing, and mentioned Bagheera's desire to interfere. May willingly volunteered be their Florence Nightingale. "It'll be an interesting veterinary project," she said, "just to see if we can do it." Thank you so much, May.

The sluggish one soon died, but the other two grew stronger and hairier day by day. As soon as May thought they were ready, we released them into the environment. One of them was introduced to campus along the Olentangy River, and the other to my porch roof.

The squirrel must have made a nest nearby, as I often saw it out my kitchen window. Bagheera continued her interest through the glass. It chattered at me sometimes while I ate breakfast, flicking its curly tail around. And I talked to the squirrel, "You be careful out in that road, Curly!"

The Party

In August, Sid and Karl decided to open up their house for an evening and invite a crowd of people from the neighborhood and beyond. They spent time planning and putting a lot of great food together. Sid set up a small table with a varied array of intoxicants in his front hallway. Karl, who was not a drinker, had coffee and a Shirley Temple bar upstairs.

Karl turned his attic into a small theater for a continuous slide show. I contributed a reel of my slides with lots of photos of people who might be there watching. I thought it would be fun to take portraits of party wildlife, and set up an area on the porch for the purpose, with lights and my antique view camera. Think Mathew Brady here.

When the evening came, I talked Les into going with me. He thought it might be of sociological interest and amusement, clearly viewing himself as an outsider. But he said, "Let me put on some decent threads first." We noticed the sky clouding up on our way down the street. Things were well under way when we arrived, just a few houses from ours. Sid's living room was overtaken by musical squatters with guitars, banjos, and fiddles, looking like they wouldn't budge from the spot all night. Les and I, both good musicians, stood in the doorway listening to the amateurs for a while, neither of us venturing in.

One of the players was my wife's breakfast mate at Marie's when our *trial* separation began. I nudged Les. "Let's get a drink and see what Karl's up to," I said. He frowned with furrowed brow and nodded his head.

On the way to the stairs, a buxom young lass, with too much cleavage showing, squeezed by me, even though it wasn't a tight space. She kind of pushed her breasts against me as she went by. "Pardon me," she said, smiling sweetly up at me. Yes it was, in fact, the very same nymph who did exactly the same thing to me at Crazyhorse early in the summer. I still wasn't impressed, but Sid must have returned without me to make another conquest. The man was insatiable, and so was she, apparently.

It was ostensibly the same party, upstairs and downstairs, but night and day in its ambiance. Soft classical music greeted us at the top of the stairs with revelers quietly exchanging pleasantries. A mixed assemblage, but a couple of young men slow danced in front of the stereo.

"A number of gay folk here," Les whispered to me.

"Well, sure," I whispered back. "Karl, you know..."

"No," Les smiled, "I didn't."

"There's a slide show in the attic if you'd like," I said. "Probably where Karl is." We ascended the remaining steps to semi-darkness and large black and white images changing on one wall. There were several chairs and a sofa, all occupied, with a few more bodies on the Oriental rug dominating the floor. We greeted Karl.

"Good timing," Karl said. "I was just starting to show some of the photographs I'm going to exhibit downtown next month. It's a group show with two other photographers."

"The opening is circled on my calendar," I said. Les and I sat on the rug, which I thought I might have seen before. "Did you ....?" I started to ask, pointing down? Les nodded and shrugged.

Karl's square format black and whites were stark and captivating. He said he hoped they spoke for themselves, but launched into a narrative about where, how, and why he made each one. Les excused himself after a dozen slides and returned two floors down to the drinks at ground zero. I stayed for the rest of the exhibit photos and some of the people pics from the next reel, the one I brought. Then I remembered I was going to take some portraits on the porch and went down myself.

The Boys were in the first floor kitchen and I stopped to ask what's new. Arthur told me there was a house for sale several doors down from the one they rented and he was thinking about putting a bid on it. "A crazy commitment," he said "It's either really smart or really stupid."

"He'll have at least one tenant," Wayne said, raising his hand. "And I've got news, too!" Then he said slowly, emphasizing each word, "I am in the vet school starting this September!" I clinked my glass with his and Art's to toast the announcements.

Out on the porch, I saw there wasn't as much light as I thought. Distant thunder came to my ears along with a camera vibrating breeze. I decided to put my portable photo studio back in the box for another day. As I was finishing, *soon to be ex* arrived with a guy I never met. She stopped on the porch, but he smiled at her and made a drinking motion with his hand and continued inside.

I stopped imagining strangling her by then, so I just said "Hey."

She had gotten a permanent, a bush of tight little curls. I knew several women who got perms after breakups. It was an interesting phenomenon, I thought. Guys, on the other hand, get an ear pierced. That's what I did a week before, thinking a small, subtle stud would symbolize a progressive attitude. Two days later, I went out and bought the largest silver ring I could find which I was sporting now, a regular pirate.

She watched me put the last pieces in the box and asked, "Whatcha doin'?"

"Thought I'd take my photo shit home while I'm still sober and ambulatory," I said.

"Mind if I go, too?" she asked. "Haven't seen your apartment."

"I don't mind," I answered. After four years together, it was easy to feel normal with her. We walked the short way up the street chattering about something, I have no idea what. Up in The Loft, I set the box on my trunk. She stood in the middle of the room, looking out my three walls of windows as lightening flashed.

"Well," she said, "Isn't this cozy?" She put her arm around my waist, standing beside me. "I do miss you," she said. I put my arm around her shoulders. There was a tie between us that might always be there, I thought. If she decided right then, that she made a mistake and wanted to stay, and I mean forever, I would probably have said yes. It could have been a very romantic moment with the storm energy around us. Rain began tapping on my roof.

"Oh, shit!" she said, turning toward the stairs, "Now I'll get wet going back to the party!"

"Here," I said, reaching behind the door for my umbrella and handing it to her. "Leave it at Sid's."

"Aren't you coming?" she asked.

"I'll be over later," I said. But I wasn't. Her hard shoes echoed down my old wooden stairwell as thunder rolled across the sky above.

Exhibitions

Sid came up to The Loft early the evening of Karl's exhibit opening. We planned to go together and he thought we should be getting there sooner than later. Sid had his psychologist's eye on Karl and wanted to help him cope with the stress of the event. "The man didn't sleep all night," he said, "and he was downright shaky this morning. I offered him a tranq, but he wouldn't take it."

"Maybe you should take it," I said, seeing how agitated he was. While we talked, I changed clothes a couple times. Recent life events had caused me to lose so much weight, nothing in my closet seemed to fit. A wardrobe adjustment was on my *to do* list.

When we got to the gallery, Karl was indeed wringing his hands nervously and pacing the hardwood floor in front of his photographs. They were attractive, tastefully framed, and well illuminated by track lights from above. The gallery space looked to be an old warehouse, nicely refinished, spacious with high ceilings.

I could tell that one of Karl's issues was a feeling of intimidation. One of the other photographers had huge, movie-poster sized images. They were abstract and colorfully splashy, expensively framed, and filled half the gallery. When we first came in, we met the photographer who was quite flamboyant in behavior and attire.

The third exhibitor was a young woman showing medium sized florals reminiscent of Georgia O'Keefe. We met her, too, a self-possessed art educator at a high school in the Columbus area.

Coach and I complimented Karl on how professional his display looked. He expressed concern that his work might be dwarfed and unnoticed next to the colorful immensity across the room. I pointed out that there was no way the guy printed those monsters himself, nor framed them either. "And look at him!" I said, "He's an asshole! You and your art have way more class."

The public arrived, a few at a time, and quickly filled the place, including many from our Northwood gang. Karl settled down and even enjoyed himself as the opening progressed. I noticed that *Salvador Dali*, across the room, sold one of his monstrosities and suggested to Sid that selling some photographs would really bolster

Karl's ego. "If we can do it anonymously, that's something you and I could do," I said.

"By God!" Sid said, "You are so right!" We walked through Karl's photos again, deciding which one we wanted, and looked around to find the gallery director. We secured a nameless purchase and made a down payment, scheduling pick-up after the month-long show. Karl told us later that several pieces had sold, looking very pleased with the whole affair.

At one point in the evening I ran into *still legally my wife,* arm in arm with another new face. She briefly told me our papers were ready to sign. "Someone told me," Sid said, after she moved on, "that she's very *easy*." I looked at him. "Oh, no!" he said, putting an arm around my shoulder, "Not me, Bro! Friendship is more important than sex!"

Goodnight, Irene

My life coach, Sid, gave me a pep talk earlier in the evening, but now that I was wandering around Dick's Den after a game of eight ball with Mack, my stomach was uneasy. I looked around at all the women who were there and wondered if any of them felt as desperate for a warm body as I did. There were some instant turn-offs, like gum chewing, purple hair, and skull tattoos, which made me think this would be a process of elimination from the start. I also noticed at least one play for pay gal who was looking for someone just like me. A distinct need had come over me lately, but I wasn't interested in finding a life partner at that moment and other avenues looked very complicated. Sid made meeting women sound so easy. "Let them do all the talking," he said, "All you have to do is get them started."

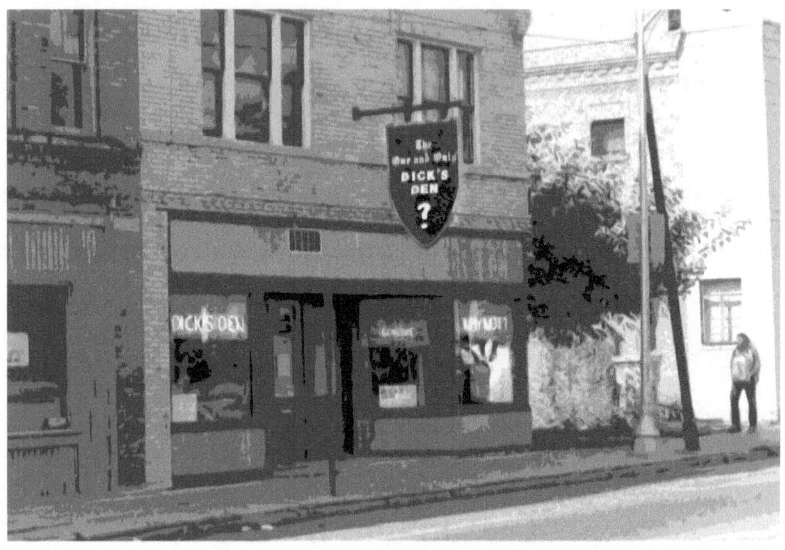

A prospect in the neighborhood of my age and sitting alone at the bar caught my attention. The parts of her that weren't hidden under a long coat looked attractive in my half-sober state. I imagined that she just got off work and was having a quick one before going home to feed her cats. But I would never know if I didn't stop imitating a statue. Taking a cleansing breath, I sat on the stool next to her. She smiled warmly at me.

"You look like..." I started.

"I came here alone," she finished, "Just got off work at the bank."

Oh great, I thought, she's a sentence finisher. "What's your..."

"Irene," she said, a preemptive question answerer, too. She opened her coat a tad and showed me her name tag from the bank. It read: My name is Irene and I'm here to help.

It disturbed me a little, but purple hair walked by just then and I wasn't going there. "I'm Rick," I said, and after a pause, "Can I..."

"Buy me a drink?" she smiled again, "Sure, I could use another. Nice to meet you, Rick."

I saw she was at the end of her scotch and held up a finger for the bartender. "The lady and I will have some scotch on th...."

"Johnny Walker," she finished.

Now, wait a minute. Finishing sentences is one thing, but I'd known this woman less than five minutes and she was finishing, correcting, and costing me an extra buck-fifty! Our drinks came and as we began to sip them she started again, "What do you...."

"I work for a sign company," I finished, "I'm a rookie so far, but looking to get into the artsier aspects of it." Her smile came back, but with a question in it. Was this the sentence finisher she longed for?

"Do you come..."

"I'm a regular," I said, "They have a sweet pool table back there." I pointed. "I'm pretty good at that." Her smile left. She fished around in her purse and came up with a small bottle of aspirin. "Do you..." I started.

"Have a headache?" she finished, "Not just yet, but, then again, I'd rather not." We reached the end of our Johnny Walkers. I yawned. "I guess it's..." she began.

"Getting kind of late," I ended, nodding. Her brows moved downward. She could dish it out, but couldn't take it.

"I think I'm about ready ...." she said.

"Me too," I replied, nodding. We slowly came to adieu and gently shook hands the way a man and a woman with no animosity do.

I was glad I hadn't driven to Dick's. The walk home felt good. I needed the fresh air. And the solitude.

Who Are We?

Mary opened our counseling session predictably. "Have you been....?" she started.

"Meeting any new women?" I finished. "Not that I'd care to see again. I'm giving that up for a while. It should be a more natural process than I'm making it."

"No need to rush. Are you isolating yourself?" she asked.

"Not at all," I said, "It's just that...." I tried to find some words.

"Hmmmm?" Mary encouraged me with the McFreud look over the rim of her spectacles. "Let me into your process."

"Did you know," I exploded, "That four or five years age difference can make a generation gap? I thought that took a *generation*, but not so!" I told Mary about my most recent encounter with a female of my species. We met through a circle of acquaintance and then found each other on the sidewalk at the youthful end of High Street. An attractive art student, she came up to The Loft on an artsy pretense. She looked a little uncomfortable, so I turned on the stereo and set the needle down on *Magic Bus,* because that was the album on the turntable.

She wrinkled her nose and asked, "Who?"

I thought she was making a little joke, so I said, "yeah!"

Then she asked, "What?"

I saw confusion on her face, so I picked up the album cover and pointed to the words *The* Who. She leafed through some of the albums by my stereo and asked if I had Abba. I could see in a flash that we would never even approach when, where, and why. She looked down at Bagheera rubbing against her leg and said she was allergic to cats. I thought that might be an excuse to escape, which it was shortly after.

Mary was laughing and had to use one of her own tissues. "Humor is a good way to process some things," she said, "Your wife is probably having similar experiences since leaving the steady comfort of your marriage." Mary was very good. Even though I could see how she manipulated our conversation, it worked.

"Listening to her, you'd think steady comfort and security were the reasons for wanting out!" I said "We signed papers, yesterday, so it's ex-wife, now."

"How do you feel about that?" she asked.

"I've been seeing her in a different way lately," I said. "She seems to wear self-assurance to hide vulnerabilities. She was strange at my friend's art exhibit a couple weeks ago."

"Tell me about that," Mary said.

"It's hard to feel sorry for people who hurt you," I said, "But I saw her standing in front of a print, using technical art terms she'd heard me use, trying to sound all sophisticated, but showing that she didn't know what the terms meant. Anyone who knew something could see she was a complete phony! I could have taken pleasure in that or I could have rescued her, but it only made me sad."

"Those are mixed emotions," she said. "Do you think you could get hold of the dominant one?"

"She was also at the neighborhood softball game, last Saturday, on the other team," I continued. "Acting like she was in total control, but she can't throw or even catch the ball and it looked like her first attempt ever at bat. I suppose sadness was my strongest feeling then."

"That reminds me of some of the things you've said about your abusive brother," Mary was clearly fishing, but that was alright.

"Speaking of people who hurt you," I said. "Yeah, he's a big clumsy oaf, the china shop bull. He acts all superior, though, and puts everyone around him down. He even gives everyone a diminutive name, like Ricky for mine. He's Gulliver and everyone else is Lilliputian. But, sure, he's easily threatened. I know that's why he does it. That doesn't make his victims hurt any less." I spit out.

"So what?" she said, "He's a jerk. Why can't you say: *So what?*"

I thought about it for a long minute. "I'm his only brother in life," I said. "I don't understand why he doesn't like me."

"That's good," Mary said, "But you're still talking about him. We want to understand you." She casually pulled the empty chair over. "Tell him why you don't need his love and approval."

"Ha!" I laughed. "You don't think that's going to work twice, do you?"

"If you let it," she said seriously. "Go ahead and tell him. Use an *I* statement."

I looked at the empty chair. "I don't ever want to be like you," I said. "You must be very unhappy."

"That's blocking. This is not about him. It's about you. Try it like this," she said, "I don't need you're approval because..."

Words welled in my chest. "I don't need your approval because," I started, feeling my guts tighten in a knot, "because I *know* I have value." I forced out the words and my body relaxed.

"Yes, wonderful!" Mary exclaimed! "It's music! Tell him again. Tell *yourself*!" She handed me the tissue box.

"I have value, dammit!" I said more easily, wiping my eyes. "Could it be that simple?"

"Some of the most profound things are simple." she said. "It's time to give up the idea that you're not smart. You are one of the big boys in this world. Try that on, wear it for a while and see how it fits!"

I blew my nose. "Alright," I said. "And I'll start saying '*so what*' to the jerks. I'm sure that will feel good."

The Empty House

There was that petite, familiar-looking woman again. Who was she? Then a circle turned in my mind and I knew. Before my wife was my wife, I hitch-hiked on the occasional weekend to visit her at Kent State, sometimes staying in the dorm room of her roommate, Hazel's, boyfriend, Jacob. An economics major, he would go on and on excitedly about trends in the stock market after we smoked some pot together, but we got along anyway, because he played the banjo and we connected over some duets. Hazel and Jacob married a few years later and we attended the wedding. "Are you shitting me!?" we said to each other when we arrived at the address on the invite. It was a multi-million dollar mansion on a bluff overlooking Lake Erie in the wealthiest of Cleveland communities. It was owned, we soon learned, by Jacob and his seventeen cousins, many of whom we met that day. There was old money in a previous generation.

A year later, Jacob came to Columbus on business and stayed a few days with us on Hudson Street. We were out one afternoon, when Jacob asked if we could stop and visit his cousin, Carly, who lived nearby. I vaguely remembered meeting her at the wedding and this second introduction confirmed my first impression that Carly was more than a little unusual. Now, a few years after that and looking out my window, I recognized the woman walking into her house. "Oh my God!" I said to Bagheera, "That's Jacob's cousin Carly living right across the street from us!" After a brief therapy session with myself, I got a grip on my shyness and walked over to knock on her door.

She owned the house which had two floors and an attic. All the rooms on the two floors were beautifully furnished and immaculately clean. There were nice antiques, paintings on walls, and beds made with lovely quilts, but there was no sign of human activity anywhere. Carly lived in the attic. The rest of the house was uninhabited and felt like a museum walking through it.

When I knocked, I heard a distant "Come in, it's open." I opened the door and saw her smiling angelically down at me from the top of the stairs. "C'mon up," she said pleasantly. There were no chairs in the attic, just some mattresses pushed together with lots of pillows and blankets. A huge German Sheppard named Vishnu got up and gave me the once-over with his nose and decided I was alright. Then he lumbered over and plopped down next to Carly, just in case I wasn't. "Take off your shoes and join me," she said, "I'm making tea."

"I just remembered who you are," I said, hoping my feet didn't smell.

"Who I am?" she asked, "I've spent my whole life trying to figure that out!"

"You're Jacob's cousin!" I said, "We met at Hazel and Jacob's wedding."

"Really?" she said, searching my face. "I don't remember you."

She wasn't wearing much, just T-shirt and shorts, and I saw deep scars peeking out here and there, including one that ran from under her hair, down the side of her neck, and into her shirt.   Not disfiguring, she was a beautiful woman inside and out. She was walking on a city sidewalk when an out of control car spun off the road and slammed into her. When the ambulance arrived, she was strapped to a board and spent some time in a hospital getting pieced back together. Then came nursing home rehab, physical therapy and Yoga, her saving grace. When she returned home, she left everything the way it was before the accident and moved into the attic with Vishnu.

I was lying on my side, sipping tea, when she made a startled sound. "Your buckle!" she said. I had an oval brass belt buckle on my jeans, etched with a simple landscape of pine trees along a river, with mountain and moon behind. Carly opened the sketchbook next to her. "I just drew this!" Her drawing was indeed a landscape in an oval, a somewhat different composition, but close enough to be spooky. "I must have known you were coming!" she said.

"I want to give you a book," she said, walking on her knees to the bookcase. She wrote an inscription inside the cover and handed it to me. It was *Be Here Now* by Baba Ram Das, a spiritual guide to living in the moment. That appeared to be the way Carly lived, appreciating each day, like so many who have faced death and survived.

"Thank you so much!" I said. It was a popular book in the late 60's, but I never got around to reading it. Vishnu got up again and lumbered slowly to me, this time licking my face all over while I scratched his neck. Gee, thanks, Vishnu. I wiped off saliva with my handkerchief.

"I don't remember how we met," she said, seriously, "but I know that you're kind, caring, and I can always trust you."

Wow! Those were things I wasn't sure I knew about myself! "How do you know all that?" I quietly asked.

"Vishnu told me!" A big smile spread across her face.

Irreconcilable Pets

Carly might have been relationship material for me, but it looked like she already had a lot of gentleman callers. She wasn't exactly the female version of Sid, but seemed to have a similar revolving door policy, maybe for different reasons. Perhaps the two of them should be together, but then, he's a psychologist and she's a little crazy. I mean that in the nicest possible way. Crazy would be fine with me, because that would make two of us.

I loved her, for sure, but wasn't *in love* with her. If we became intimate, that might happen, but then where would we be? I'd want her all to myself and, if it didn't work out, it would be difficult to avoid such a close neighbor. Relationships were so very complicated in my mind. Why did Sid think having four girlfriends simultaneously wasn't complicated? It puzzled me.

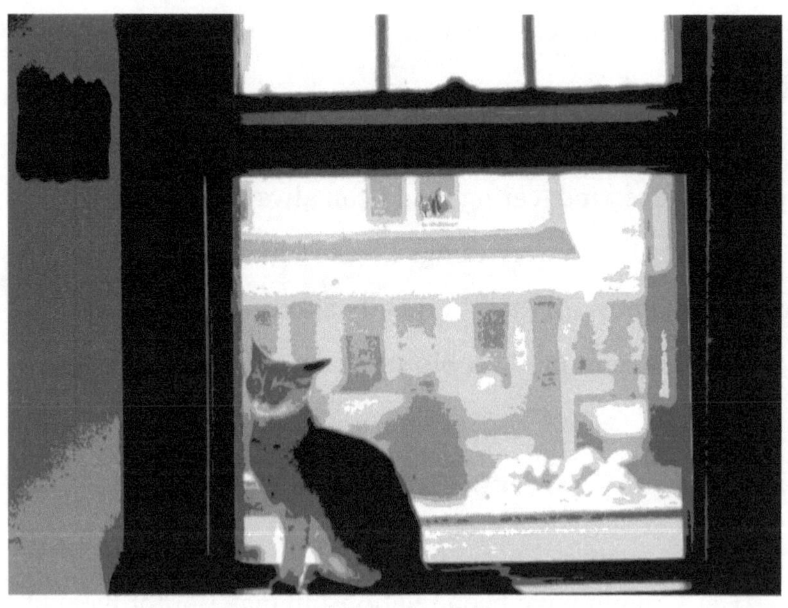

Carly was always welcoming when I visited her attic and we had pleasant exchanges on the street between our abodes, but the one and only time she and Vishnu walked up to The Loft, it was a disaster. Vishnu came slowly up my stairs after Carly, but just as he reached the top, Bagheera leapt out of the kitchen and attacked him!

She spat at him, hissed, and jumped at his face with a furious flurry of claws, scratching the hell out of him.

I threw a coat over the cat, picked her up, and tossed her into the bedroom, closing the door. Vishnu retreated to the landing half-way up and lay down wining. Carly and I went down and spent a long time consoling and caressing him, but he wouldn't take another step upward.

After a while, Carly and I went up to the living room and sat on the sofa, hoping Vishnu might reconsider and join us. We tried to have a friendly visit, but the vivid animal kingdom display we just witnessed cast a shadow and it wasn't long before she and Vishnu went back across the street.

Working Class Blues

The sign shop building was divided into two main sections of equivalent size, the art side and the construction side. The artsy side was cleaned and swept at closing time every evening by the people working there, each in their respective niche. The lettering easels, darkroom, screen-print shop, paste-up drawing table, and a central room for materials were all in that area, as well as the office and customer reception room. It was well vented but had an air of paint and various thinners, a pleasurable aroma to artsy types.

While I was waiting for my job interview, Ray, the owner, was verbally reaming someone a new asshole for using one of his twenty dollar oil brushes and returning it without thoroughly cleaning it. After he hired me, the first time I used one of his brushes, I returned it in cleaner condition than when I got my hands on it. I'm a quick learner. That put me on his good side and I intended to stay there.

Half a dozen rough sorts worked on the construction side, The Brothers not the worst of them. There was a jigsaw, table saw, sand-blasting room, spray paint booth, and an 8' x 12' oven and vacuum press to make plastic faces for lighted signs. The sign erection bucket or *boom* truck was parked inside that area at night. It was a filthy, dusty, noisy workplace that smelled of gasoline, oil, and melted plastic.

Tension and animosity arose occasionally between the workers in the two very different areas. I was the young rooky on the artsy side, so it was me if an extra hand was needed on the dirty side or out at an erection site. One morning I was about to start in on some real estate signs ahead of schedule, when Ray asked me to help Chip repair a sign on a law firm building that reportedly had become unsecure. The Brothers would usually be doing this, but they were off on another important erection job. "I'm sorry," my boss said, "Hopefully it won't take long."

The worst of it was working with Chip. He was a disheveled, vulgar, baboon, who was openly racist and sexist. And he was an ignorant moron, too. I didn't like him, can you tell? A couple weeks earlier, Chip realized too late that he left out the second *i* in *prescription* on two plastic sign faces he made for a

drugstore. Can you even believe he thought no one would notice?
The idiot charged ahead and sprayed stencil film on them, cut out
the letters, spray painted them, installed them in the aluminum
fixture, and was loading the finished sign onto the truck. We're
talking about six hundred dollars in materials and two days' work.

It was lunch time and all of us on the artsy side, including
Ray, were sitting at the picnic table outside the office door watching.
Mark noticed it first and began a squealing outburst of attempted
communication which no one understood. Then he turned to me and
signed, "Wrong spelling." The others looked at me for interpretation
and I said, "It's spelled wrong!" We all turned to see and groaned in
unison, except Ray, who completely lost it and screamed
obscenities. Honestly, why didn't he fire the fool on the spot?

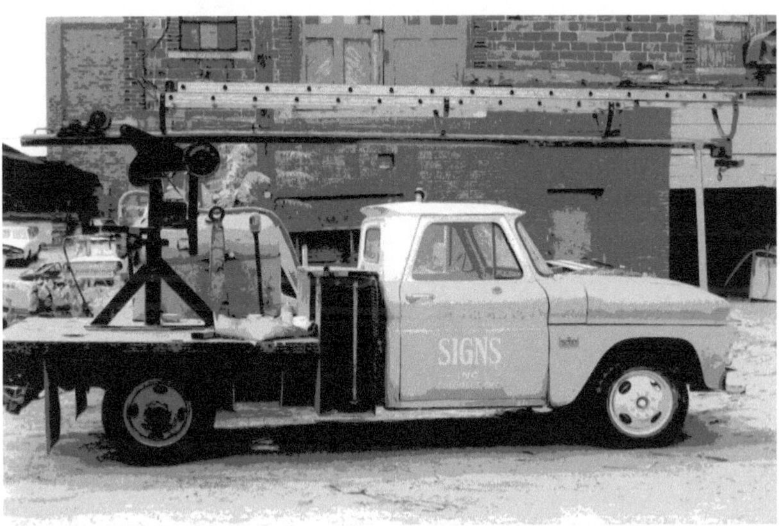

So I'm riding in the truck to fix a sign with Chip, trying to stay calm and not listen to him spew out his fascist view of the world. He held his hand like a pistol and pretended to shoot people as we drove along: blacks, Hispanics, Asians, etc. And I was the one seeing the talking doctor!

The law firm sign was indeed listing about twenty feet above the sidewalk on the eave of the building and vibrating a bit in the breeze. Summer was changing to autumn with a chill in the air. We set ladders up to either end of it and climbed to the top. "Oh, man," I said, "The roof is rotten over here."

"So, what?" he said.

"So, there's nothing wrong with the sign," I said, "What these guys need is a building contractor, not us."

"Our boss and the customer expect us to straighten this thing and that's what we're going to do!" he said, "You climb on the roof and I'll get some plywood from the truck to reinforce it."

"Climb on the roof!" I said, "I am not suicidal. They're lawyers! They'll understand the situation and they want to know if their roof is rotting."

"I'm in charge, here," he barked, "And you'll do what I tell you!"

That was all I needed to hear. I climbed down the ladder and started walking.

"Hey!" he shouted, "Where the hell are you going?"

At the corner, a bus was taking on passengers. I got on without even seeing where it was going. Any other place would do.

My pulse returned to normal after a few slow deep breaths. Then I saw the king of clubs on the floor of the bus, no other cards around. I was studying Tarot cards at the time and the king of clubs definitely says, *you are one of the big boys in this world.* I picked it up and put it in my pocket.

When I saw where the bus was going, I got a transfer and hopped another to get back to the sign shop. I carefully explained the rotten roof to Ray, leaving out the part about Chip being a dunce. There was no need. The drugstore sign was still fresh in Ray's memory. He agreed with me, said he was glad *someone* had common sense, and put his jacket on to go see for himself. A few weeks later he let Chip go. Thank you, Ray.

I began to relax, walking back to my safe, secure, darkroom, or dark *womb* perhaps, to make my realty printing screens.

Emotions

Mary and I sat down for our weekly session, but I found very little to say at first. I glanced at her third chair a couple times.

Abruptly, she lifted her foot to the chair and shoved it to the other side of her small office. "That's just an empty chair," she said. "Let's be done with him for a while."

"Amen, Mary," I affirmed. One small gesture and I was almost ready for her tissue box. But instead, I launched into an evening I had over the weekend.

Lucky Penny

Sid performed at the Cockroach Coffeehouse, a popular underground venue on High Street. I think it cost fifty cents to get in and coffee was ten cents, *instant* I'm pretty sure. Of course there were no windows and the lighting was terrible. The regulars brought small pillows because there were no chairs. Everyone sat on the floor; a cold, cement, basement floor. Sound inviting? It was all about the folk music performers who sat on low stools above the audience.

Les and I tiptoed around people until we found a small square of unoccupied floor. I saw Les play in public once. He tried to be the best musician he could, a little nervous before going on, but did a great job. Afterward, I complimented him. "Fantastic improv on that last number!" I said.

"You heard it!" Les exclaimed! "I bet you're the only one." It was a youthful gathering and Les thought they were more into dance and romance than music, feeling unappreciated. He was self-conscious about getting on stage, but wanted people to listen when he did. Les tried to hide them, but he was full of feelings.

At The Cockroach, Sid's set was more about words than music. He wasn't a great guitarist, but neither was Bobby Dylan. Sid's lyrics evoked a heartfelt response from his listeners. I was choked up and saw others were moved.

"I could never do that," I said to Mary, relating this whole Cockroach scene to her.

"You say you're a guitarist, yourself, though I haven't heard you play," she said. "Not everyone is a performer. What is your reason?"

"I was pushed on stage a lot as a kid. Making music for the joy of it was good, but not in front of a crowd. Now I get nervous just watching someone else perform!" I'd been mulling something else over, thinking it might be a sought-after epiphany. "And I can't sing an emotional song, even when I'm alone!" I said. "There's always a lump in my throat and a tear in my eye. Even without any lyrics, beautiful music by itself can hit me hard."

"And how does your friend overcome his feelings?" she asked.   "Is he disingenuous?"

"Oh, No, I don't think so." I replied. "They are his words. He writes these songs. It's like he has the ability to elicit an emotional response from his listeners, but stoically, without having the response himself."

"*Another* thing you admire about him," she commented. Mary was so good, skillfully drawing me into Sid's way with women. "Is he disingenuous with his many girlfriends?"

"I don't know," I went over it in my mind. "Maybe he's singing like that to draw more of them to his bed!" I laughed. "But, I suppose he could *think* he loves them all." Then I felt sad. "Someone's feelings must get hurt."

"And you don't want to do that." she stated.

I thought I had all this worked out, but my vision crumbled. "It's like the music. I have strong feelings for people. If I didn't care about someone, I couldn't get in bed with them. And whether or not I cared, I wouldn't want to hurt them."

"That's very reasonable and human," she said, "But isn't there more to it? What is it that makes you so human?"

"It's because," I began, but felt that lump in my throat.

"Come on," Mary said, "Don't hold it in." She gave me *the look.* "Give me an *I* statement."

"Because," I tried again. "Because I know how it feels!" I took a deep breath and blew it out. "I really know how that feels. People can be so thoughtless and cruel to each other."

Yet, again, she handed me tissues, smiling. "I'm so glad you're not going to be a womanizer."

Stability

Winter came, and everything in my life seemed somewhat right, or at least better. The Loft was like home, with my affectionate cat purring around me and friendly neighbors on all sides. There was a little less evening carousing and more art projects getting worked on. My world was predictably stable at the moment, which made me feel less crazy.

At the sign shop, there was a lot of work to keep me busy without being called upon by the erection crew, thank you so much. Ray said it was because word got around that I was doing quality screen printing. It was the perfect time to ask for a raise and I got a nice one.

The lettering staff was also getting a lot of work, with a new hire and Ray, himself, frequently wielding his brushes. The new one was Tess, a young lady a few years older than me, I guessed. Mark told me she had an MFA degree from somewhere and was doing a good job. "But slow," he signed. "Ray will want her to work faster. This is not art school."

Several days after Tess arrived, I was silently asking Mark in sign language about a particular job. Tess turned to look and then back to her lettering. "You are so cute!" she said emphatically!

It stopped me. "I beg your pardon?" I asked.

She spun around and put a hand to her throat. "Oh!" she said, "I thought you were deaf!"

Mark read her lips and laughed. "I see her watching you," he signed with raised eyebrows, warning me.

"I'm so embarrassed!" Tess said, "But it's your fault! You're so quiet! I only see you talking with your hands to Mark."

We introduced ourselves. There was a folksy air about her. We both came from small town Ohio on either side of the state. She was an easy person to be around. One of The Brothers already hit on her. She laughed about it.

"They're not bad guys," I said, "Just a little rough around the edges." It looked like we had a lot in common, but it was time to get back to work.

On Friday afternoon, Ray knocked on the darkroom door to tell me my ex-wife was on the phone. "You won't believe why," he warned me, shaking his head. I slowly walked to the phone, wishing I didn't have to.

"The car burned up, Honey!" my ex said, "I don't know what to do."

Her car was only a few years old. I took great care of it when we were together; doing all the regular maintenance and some repairs myself. "What could have happened?" I asked.

"It sounded terrible!" she said, "And then it was smoking and caught on fire."

Upon further questioning, she admitted that the oil light had been on for many months. "We call those *idiot lights*," I said. It was not my problem, but offered some suggestions for her next step.

When I hung up, I saw Ray and Mark laughing and joined them. It was funny in a dark sort of way, to be amused by someone else's problems. Schadenfreude is what the Germans call it.

"A divorcee, huh?" Tess asked.

"Yeah!" I said, "And single is looking pretty good right now." That brought on another fit of laughter, before we all got back to work.

At closing time, Tess asked me if I wouldn't mind taking her home. Her car was getting fixed and she took the bus that morning. "I wanted to take my art kit and some paper home for the weekend," she said. She called me 'Ricky', which I usually react negatively to because my brother used the name to make me less significant. But falling from the lips of Tess, it was the opposite; a playful attempt at intimacy. I liked the sound of it suddenly.

When she told me where she lived I realized it was only a few blocks from my place. I drove by Northwood and pointed out The Loft on our way. She had an upstairs apartment, like mine, and I helped schlep her stuff up the stairs. Her apartment was one big room with a high ceiling. Some of her artworks were around: very realistic pencil work and paintings of comfortable interiors. Tess was way ahead of me in her ability to say what she wanted with art.

"I could make dinner for us," she suggested, kind of drawing an imaginary picture on the front of my sweatshirt with her finger.

"Well," I began, "Thanks so much, but I'd like to go home, feed my cat, and take a shower. I smell like paint."

We were standing close and had a friendly little kiss. I must have initiated it because I'm a foot taller. But then she pulled my face to hers for a kiss that was the real thing.

"I....um," I stammered, "I like you, but I'm not ready to fall into bed with you."

Tess laughed at me as we walked to the door. Then she looked at me smiling. "Maybe tomorrow," she said and playfully pushed me out the door.

Stability is an illusion.

Tomorrow Comes

The next day came and I spent much of it working on ideas for screen prints. Now that I was a stable, productive employee, Ray said I could use the shop after hours and Saturdays to make my own art prints, thank you Ray.

At dusk I was thinking about wandering over to Dick's, but Tess was walking over to my place at the same time. I was about to put on my jacket when I heard her voice downstairs and poured myself a glass of wine instead. After a few minutes, she came up to The Loft.

"I just met Les and Jill," she said. "They're stoned."

"Well," I shrugged, "It *is* Saturday night."

She went into my living room and frowned, saying, "Your ceiling is black." So far, only the Big Dipper and North Star graced it. Then she took in the downward view of street and neighborhood from my windows. "Cool!" she said. "I'll trade you, Ricky." My art projects were lying around and she looked through them, just as I had the night before at her place. "Everyone sees the world differently," she commented.

I was sipping my wine and offered her something. She didn't drink, smoke pot, or do whatever the hell Les and Jill were doing. "But there are some other ways to get high," she said. I thought she might be referring to sex, but she wasn't. Then she started drawing on my chest with her finger again, while softly humming a pleasant melody. "I locked your door when I came up," she half-whispered.

Surrender was in my heart and we quickly found our way to the bedroom. It was as normal and natural as sex could be. We slept peacefully entwined through the night and woke to morning light with Bagheera purring softly on top of us. It felt like we'd been together for years, but we didn't know a whole lot about each other. Was *chemistry* enough? My wife and I had chemistry: sulfuric acid meets caustic soda.

We had breakfast at the kitchen table and that was very comfortable, too. Tess, a vegetarian, enjoyed my granola from the food co-op. Curly jumped down to the roof, chattering outside the window, and I related my squirrel story. I recently made a small feeding box, and put nuts and cracked corn in it when snow covered the ground.

After that night, we were together regularly to share a meal or walk in the park, and shared a bed a few nights a week. That's when we started getting to know each other in that other way. I don't know what she saw, but I wasn't going to hide my phobias and self-doubt from her.

As for my perspective, Tess meditated a lot. I'm into Yoga and no stranger to meditation, but this was unusual meditation which involved pulling a sheet over her head. "I'm OK with that," I told myself.

Her apartment was in a house owned by friends, Lance and Angel. Lance interested me, because he was an independent craftsman who made artsy things with wood and sold them at art festivals.   He also had a handyman, Mr. Fixit, thing going on in the North Columbus area.

I met other folks in their circle when I visited Tess. They used terms I wasn't familiar with. For example they called each other *premies*.

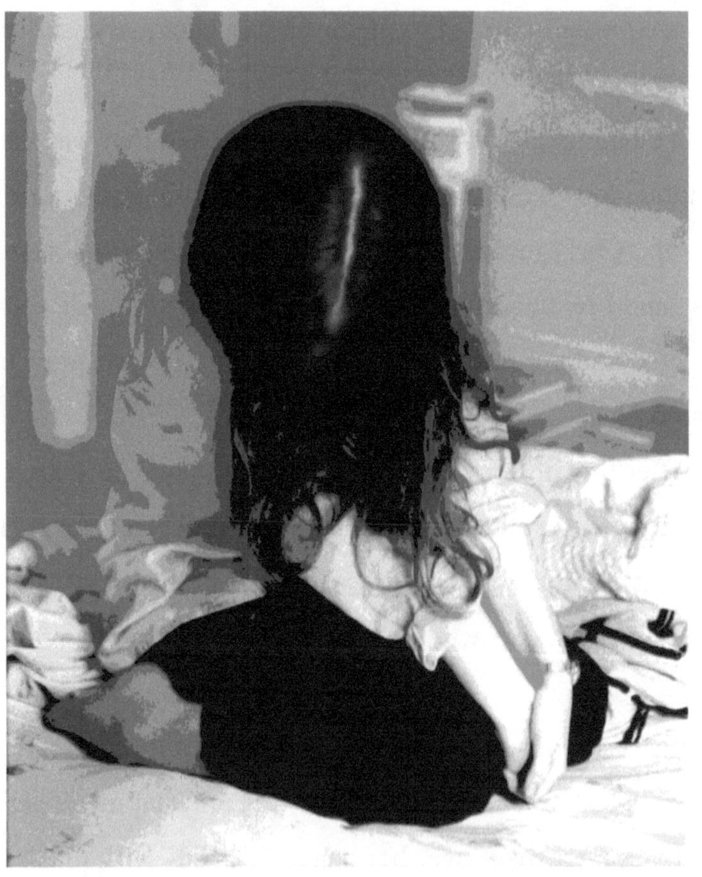

"Preemies?" I asked Tess. "Were all you people born early?"

That cracked her up, keeping my twenty-questions light. They were called premies at the ashram where they all met. It comes from a Hindi word meaning *Love* or *lovers.* They also referred to casual conversation as *satsang,* which is Sanskrit for *true company*.

I didn't get it until I saw some books and magazines in Lance and Angel's place. My stomach took a turn. Tess and her friends were in a cult that worshiped a young self-proclaimed *perfect master* from India.

Upheaval from war and social changes had a lot of people looking for some kind of truth. There were lots of cults at the time, like the Moonies, Scientology, Transcendentalism, and selling *Amway*. I'm not a religious person and I'm not sure I believe in truth, so I have problems with all these groups. Whether or not this guru was a complete fraud was irrelevant. I reject the very concept of *worship,* whether it's Jesus, Mohamed, or Marilyn Monroe. The only conclave I found comfort in was Northwood which had no bible, creed, taboo, or ritual.

I expressed my reservations about our differences with her, but she dismissed them. "Let's enjoy what we have and not worry about the future," she said. Tess and I continued our loving relationship, but I doubted it would have longevity. We kept our separate lives and never broached the subject of cohabitation. When we were together, it sometimes felt like there was a third party in the room.

Friday Night

Drying off after my Friday, post work, shower ritual, which included a bit of paint thinner I kept in the medicine cabinet, I heard someone else in The Loft. "Hello?" I asked, opening the bathroom door a crack.

The soft melancholy voice of Mack came to me. "It's just me."

When I came out with towel around me, he was studying things under magnets on my refrigerator. Bagheera sat on his shoulder. She liked him. "The King of Clubs," he said. "What's that about?"

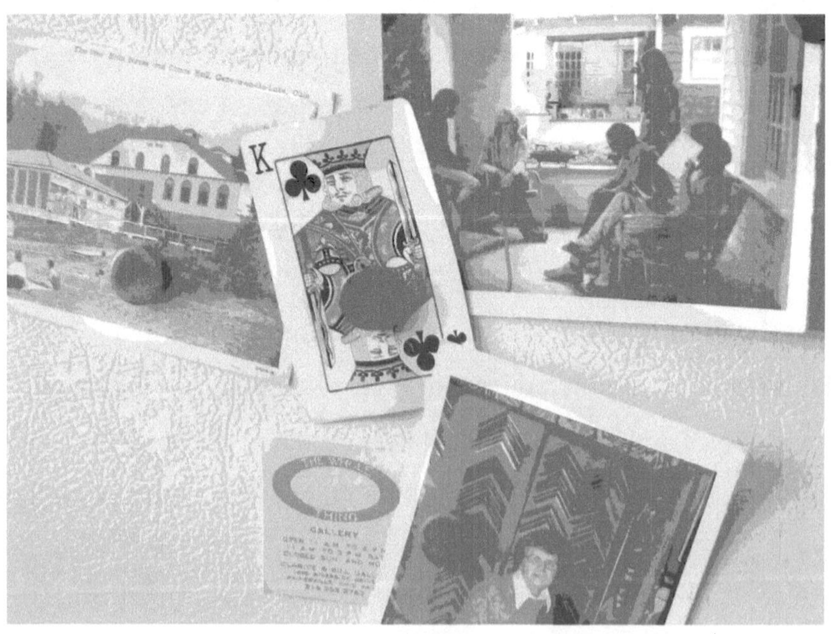

"That's my new persona," I said, "maybe." I went into the bedroom to dress.

"I like it!" he said, sounding a lot like Mary. "Maybe it's your old persona and you just don't know it." What I didn't know at the time, was that he was getting counseling at the same clinic I was.

When I rejoined him, he had progressed to the inside of my fridge and was eating a sandwich, feeding little bits to my cat. "Let's go to Dick's and play a few games," he said. *"I'll drive."*

"Why not?" I replied, which is, in fact, the Dick's Den motto, painted on their front window.

At the tavern, we were visiting with some folks on the sidewalk when I noticed Irene, the sentence finisher, through the window, sitting at the bar. "Say, Mack," I said, "is there another asylum we could go to tonight?" I turned my back to the window and pointed inside, shaking my head.

"Asylum?" he asked. There was a smile on his face, a refreshing change. "Lobo's is close," he said. "They have a couple nice pool tables."

It was January and the warmth of Lobo's was welcome after walking a couple more blocks. It was my first sojourn into the place, so I stopped just inside to drink in the atmosphere. Mack went into the back room to see about a pool table. The bar was a rectangle in the middle of the main room with small tables around the perimeter. There were a lot of people there, but the ones I noticed right away were a couple of rough, tattooed bikers sitting on the right side of the bar. I walked around to the left. In the corner was a noisy, barely legal foursome, acting their age.

Then I saw Carly, sitting alone and looking a little spacey. Well, she always had faraway eyes. I made my way over to her table and sat down. "Hey neighbor," I said.

"Rick!" she smiled. "Is this one of your hangouts?"

"First time," I said. "I was going to Dick's, but a new venue seemed like a good idea suddenly. Everything good with you?"

"Good enough," she said, looking into her glass. "Sometimes I lose my *here and now* and have to get out." She took a sip and brightened again. "You want a martini?" she asked, "I mean, like a good martini?" She opened her purse and gave me a peek at her Bombay bottle. "I order vermouth and add Bombay. It's the best, but you know that."

"Some would argue Tanqueray," I said, "but, sure, only the English know gin."

"I could tell you came from a civilized family," she said, "But Lobo's doesn't have that either."

I wondered why she went there, if she didn't like the joint. She told me it used to be a better place a long time ago. There looked to be a sadness coming over her. She used to come there with someone very special in her life.

"Didn't you used to be married?" she asked.

"Once upon a time," I said, "but not happily ever after."

Mack came over to say a table was ours in a couple minutes. "Carly, Mack," I introduced them. We excused ourselves and went to the pool room in the back.

Racking the balls, Mack asked if Carly was the Queen of Clubs. "I don't think so," I said. "She's my friend and neighbor."

"You're friends," Mack said. "That's a good start."

Barroom pool works like this: You place a buck on the pay side of the table to declare the next game. Sometimes you have to beat the winner of the previous game to gain control, but negotiations are possible. Mack put his buck down when we first came in and now it was our turn. The previous winner surrendered his stick. I refused to bet a drink on the game with Mack, and broke the rack. The game didn't last very long, and we gave up the table to the next player.

Emerging from the doorway of the pool room, Mack and I saw the bartender over at Carly's table in heated argument. He was trying to throw her out for the BYOB and she was telling him the house stuff wasn't drinkable.

Then these biker ruffians came on either arm and lifted her to her feet, saying they would take her home. She looked frightened. Suddenly, I saw myself striding across the room and putting my arm around Carly. "The lady is with me," I said firmly and calmly, feeling anything but.

"Yes, Rick," she said, looking up at me, "Let's get out of here." My heart pounded as the bartender and leather jackets backed off. I picked up Carly's purse and we moved toward the door, every eye in the place on us.

Walking down the sidewalk, I was still shaken, but Carly laughed. "Vishnu was right about you," she said. "As soon as I saw you walking toward me, I knew everything was going to turn out alright."

I sure didn't know that. "Did you drive?" I asked. "I'm a pedestrian tonight and it's freezing."

"It's on the next block," she said.

"Ready to go home?" I asked.

"Yeah," she said, laughing again. "I have my here and now back." She fished the keys out of her purse and handed them to me. "You drive," she said. "Take us back to Northwood."

Special Delivery

The Hemlocks were heavy with snow when I got home from work on Monday evening. There was a good bit on me, too, which I brushed off while stomping my boots on the porch. Among the usual bills for me and Les, the mail box had an item not delivered by our postal worker. The envelope was simply addressed to 'Rick' in a very beautiful script that I recognized at a glance. It was from the same hand that inscribed my Ram Das, *Be Here Now* book. I opened it and read the short note several times under the dim porch light with big fluffy flakes falling.

"To you, Dear Rick,

For a lovely space in time. I am grateful and so fortunate to have you in my life.

Carly "

The signature was large and so full of curvy serifs that the Palmer Cursive Writing Method I learned in school looked like crude scratches by comparison. I turned the note over and found what looked like a one-sentence poem.

Les came up the steps and kicked his shoes against the wall. "Whatcha got?" he asked, "Good news?"

"I don't know," I said, aiming it at him. "Is this a love note?

He looked it over and chuckled. "Well, it's not hate mail," he said, "And the writing is so artistic, it's suitable for a picture frame."

Jill shook snow from her stylish winter coat and pulled the faux fur hood off her head. "Let me see," she said coming to my side. She read the missive and sighed. "It's a very nice note with nothing to read between the lines." She put her arm around my waist and gave me a squeeze. "Someone likes you," she said, "Don't fight it. It's a blessing, not a curse."

I turned it over so she could see the back. Jill read aloud, "Love is a pure white butterfly."

"A white butterfly," Les repeated, thoughtfully. He unlocked the door and held it open for us. "Isn't that some kind of moth?"

Trainwreck

Elevated train tracks ran north and south on a steep hill above and behind the sign shop. A few times a day, a long slow-moving train passed, disrupting some sign making activity. The vibration put a temporary halt to copy camera use and more delicate lettering jobs. The noise was annoying, but it also created extra break time.

During one of these daily events, Tess and I were having a tense moment about our differences, outside the darkroom door. These conversations were always my fault. She lived in the moment and I envisioned the future. I was trying to go with the flow, but didn't want to be around idol worship. The moment was blessedly interrupted by a very loud crashing and the train quickly grinding to a halt.

Everyone in the shop walked out and around the building to see a tanker car, derailed and upside-down on the side of the hill. They look really huge when you're up close. It was still partly coupled with the tanker next to it, but appeared precarious, like it might break away and roll down the rest of the way, causing property damage or injury.

The sign company was located in a poor residential neighborhood, so naturally, a large crowd of folks quickly formed to gawk. Because of the familiar logo on the side of all the tankers, everyone could see the train was headed for the Bush Brewing

Company on the north end of Columbus. After ten minutes, the train hadn't budged, making one young man feel safe enough to climb up and turn the big wheel on the car's top. After a few turns, it swung open, knocking the man back down the hill. Then rice poured out: tons of long grain white rice forming a mountain of food.

Everyone ran to get collection containers, including Tess and me. There was a lot of joyful laughter, singing, and high-fives as we gathered up rice. Before authorities came and shooed people away, Tess and I had stashed a hundred pounds or more of rice in our cars. Unbelievably, I didn't photograph this beautiful scene, no Pulitzer Prize for me.

After work, I followed Tess home to help carry rice upstairs. Lance and Angel came up to see what was going on. Tess told the tale as she filled a large bag of rice for them.

Tess came back to The Loft with me, where we made a big pot of beans and rice to test it out. We invited Les and Jill to join us and, yet again, told the story.

"I always thought beer was hops and barley," Les said, "But let the truth be told. It's mostly rice!"

"A long row of tankers go there every day," I said, "I had no idea!"

Summer of Food

Despite some stumbling blocks in our relationship, Tess and I fell into a routine of together time. She wanted to be vegan, but was a vegetarian because there were so few options at our urban grocery store or the local restaurants in those days. Talita's Tacos had menu options for both our diets and became *our place* if we ate out, the booth by the window.

Sunday mornings usually found us walking along the Olentangy River through campus or the park areas north. We both came from farming communities and noted with interest the OSU agricultural school's experimental farmland right across the river. In early summer, when the Olentangy is a full swift river, we saw the young plants. A lot of it was corn, but another area, we speculated, was planted with various varieties of beans. By July, it was clear that tomatoes were growing in another part along with, we thought, the cabbage family.

Then one Sunday in early August, we saw how low the Olentangy had become and how little water was going over the small dam on the north end of campus. Carrying our shoes, we ventured across, holding hands to steady each other.

Yes, indeed, there was a whole hell of a lot of corn on the other side, and it was ripe. I took off my T-shirt, made a bag of it and we picked some for dinner. Walking further, we found the beans, and added some to the corn. Then we found tomatoes and helped ourselves to a few. Walking back across the dam was a little trickier with my stretched out shirt and Tess clutching a cauliflower to her breast. The taboo of it all added to the thrill of our day.

Back at The loft, we washed it all very well, thinking they might be experimenting with pesticides and herbicides, too. Then we had a vegetable feast and stuffed ourselves. The corn was especially fresh and delicious, compared to what was in our grocery store.

The next Sunday, we wore backpacks.

Dad

In Mary's office, I sat down for our session and pointed to her empty chair. "I have value, asshole!"

"I see you're ready, today," Mary said, chuckling.

"I am," I said, "Let's get to work!

Mary slowly turned the empty chair around, so it's back faced us. Damn, she was good. "Do you have any other difficult family relationships?" she asked.

I started going over it in my mind. "Most family relationships are a little tricky, aren't they?"

Mom and I were alright, except she might have done more to protect me. She might be the one I have most in common with, always making crafty things. I love cooking with her over the holidays. She's taught me so much in her kitchen.

"I have a sister, but she's an alien from a parallel universe where rationality doesn't exist. Never abusive, but it's second nature for her to patronize me. 'Maybe you'll understand someday, when you're more mature,' she says. I *understand* that she lives in a fantasy world and probably *still* believes in the Easter bunny!"

"Dad is a bit more complicated, I suppose," I said.

"What's he like?" Mary asked.

"You mean, in contrast to that empty chair?" I asked.

"If you like," she said, "Let's go with your father, today," She looked at me over her glasses.

"I always felt loved," I said right away, "And he never lied to me."

Those felt like the important points of *contrast*, but reflecting, I saw a lot of other positive things. Even as a little kid, I liked making things with my hands. Dad often found time to take an interest and help me with my projects. He didn't mind if I used his workshop corner in the basement and taught me how to use his tools. *Safety first* was his mantra about those. When he criticized me, it was helpful, not hurtful.

Memory is like many of our faculties, if we don't use them, atrophy sets in. When you exercise it, like a muscle, it gets stronger. As I focused on Dad, the floodgate opened.

"He's such a smart man," I told Mary, "But never understood my childhood traumas."

In second grade, after two years of moving around the country, I felt sick as soon as I walked into the school building, sometimes throwing up. The school nurse would call Mom, who came to get me. But the moment I got into the car, I felt fine. Dad dismissed all this. "It's all in your head," he said many times.

"That was the first time I started counseling," I said, "Eight years old."

"What do you remember about that?" Mary asked.

I couldn't remember much of anything. The county school psychologist had a comfortable office. We played a lot of games, drew pictures on the blackboard, and talked. I had fun when I visited her.

Dad, not getting the mental health issue, suggested I might have a *physical* health problem. Then I was seeing our family doctor, testing for various health conditions, including a brief hospital stay for a barium stomach ulcer test. That made me *more* stressful and, I suppose, angry with my dad.

The doctor couldn't find anything wrong with my body, so we sat down for a chat. He was an experienced, caring physician who asked gentle questions and listened. I tried to explain my feeling of dread about school. "I think you could talk yourself into going," he suggested, "You might be missing out on some fun stuff!"

"Not exactly Carl Rogers," I said to Mary, "But way more sensitive than *all in your head*."

"What's your relationship with your father like, now?" Mary asked.

I thought about the last few times I saw him. Their gallery business was growing, and I visited on the occasional weekend to help catch them up on customer picture framing. Dad had lost a step and the loss of confidence in his body slowed him down in other ways. It also mellowed him, making it easier to communicate things of the heart with. I still call him for advice all the time. "He's more like a friend now," I said.

Then another memory arose and hit me hard. When I was about ten, my brother stopped me at the door to my room one night. I had just given Dad a bedtime hug. "Why do you do that?" he asked, "It's not very manly!" The next night, I told Dad that bedtime hugs were kid stuff, and the saddest look came over him. I went to my room feeling terrible.

"At eighteen, I started hugging him again," I told Mary, "The hiatus made it all the more meaningful. Now, they're special moments."

Group Therapy

At the community mental health center, I joined a therapy group at Mary's urging. We met on Wednesday evenings in a large basement room. George, the therapist guiding us, was a very young man, a few years my senior. The setting was a comfy lounge-like square, with two sofas opposite and two easy chairs on each of the other sides. A large round coffee table took up the middle with little end tables at the corners, each with its own tissue box. If Mary's motive was to show me I was not alone, or that there were lots of crazier people than me, she succeeded.

There was Martha who was so quiet and shy, I strained to hear her when she spoke, which wasn't often. In contrast, June was a loudmouthed type-A who wanted to dominate the sessions.

Howard, a fidgety sort with restless-leg syndrome, had visions of killing people. "Not people I dislike, but random people for no apparent reason," he shared with us. His higher self lived in constant fear that he might cross the line and hurt someone. Especially in his car, he imagined running people over.

Dan, about my age, was in a lousy marriage and went beyond imagining. He actually tried to strangle his spouse before coming to his senses. I think he might have begun counseling under a court order. "She and I are completely incompatible," he said, "We simply have to split."

"Sounds like you have passion," June said, "You're not ignoring each other."

"Just because two people fight like cats and dogs, doesn't mean they aren't both good people," George said, "Compatibility is a real issue."

"How about you, George?" mousey Martha asked. "We've all introduced ourselves, but we don't know anything about you."

"That's right," Dan said, "Are you supposed to lead the group from, like, outside? Or will you be a participant?"

"There are different philosophies about that," George said, "Leading a group is a first for me, but I like the idea of belonging to it, if that's alright."

Everyone nodded their heads, agreeing it was the way to go.

So George gave us a brief picture of his severe, ultra-religious upbringing. He went into seminary, but soon had an anxiety reaction to it. Help was found at the mental health center. "Counseling looked like a better way to help people, so I left seminary and became a psychologist. And thank you for inviting me to participate. I feel more comfortable now."

One thing we all seemed to experience was some sort of abuse as children. When the subject came up, we had a lively discussion. Even quiet Martha angrily vented about it. I wondered if *happy childhood* was an oxymoron.

Since it was a new group, George told us to expect more members, so it was no surprise that another lunatic was introduced the next week. The surprise was that it was the guy who jumped into bed with my ex the minute I walked out the door.

"No!" I said!

He agreed, shaking his head, "This won't work. Maybe we'll be able to talk someday." He held out his hand and we had a brief shake.

I explained the situation to the group after he left. Memory is like reliving, so I was a bit shaken.

"She drives her men to therapy," June said, giving my knee a friendly pat. "I'd like to meet this woman."

"What's attractive about that?" Dan asked.

"Just kidding," June said, trying to get real with us, "I don't *think* that's who I am. As a woman I want to be empowered, but positively."

"That reminds me of something," I said, "Howard, I'm ashamed to admit it, but at our first session I formulated the impression that you were a dangerous lunatic. I realize now, that I wasn't hearing you. An image of killing my ex haunted me for a while, much like you described. I think I was feeling powerless."

"Thanks, Man," he said, "I probably didn't express myself very well that first time."

"So we've formulated perceptions of each other and of ourselves," George said, "But we can modify those as we get to know each other and, hopefully, ourselves. Part of our process can be helping each other do that. I like how this is going!"

The Survey

Bagheera meowed frantically as I prepared her dinner as fast as I could. Slow plodding footsteps sounded on my stairs. Sid came into The Loft and sprawled across my sofa, letting out a long sigh.

"Friday night?" I asked, putting Bagheera's dish on the floor, "And no ladies?"

"I'm sick of women," he replied with disgust.

"What happened?" I asked, trying to imitate the Mary McFreud *look.* No way was Casanova sick of women.

Further probing brought it out. He was in bed with a woman when the phone rang. It was the woman he had sex with the day before. He tried to say he'd call her back, but couldn't get a word in. Then his doorbell rang, so he excused himself from the caller and woman in bed, put on his robe and went to the door. It was a woman he slept with last week. She was crying. Back in the bedroom, the one in bed was arguing with the one on the phone. "This is not a normal lifestyle I'm experiencing," He said in anguish, "I've got to stop, stop, stop!

I asked him if he'd thought about getting some counseling, explaining how much help I'd gotten from my counselor, Mary *McFreud.* It's very difficult to get psychologists to take their own medicine. Sid changed the subject. His real problem of the moment was something else, he claimed.

Sid was working long and hard on his doctoral dissertation and thought it was in pretty fair shape, but couldn't get any of his Profs or fellow students to look it over. "I need some feedback," he said.

"I'll read it," I offered. Sid raised an eyebrow at me. "Just because I'm a dropout doesn't mean I wouldn't get it," I said. "I took Psych in school and I have long personal experience with counseling." I pulled a textbook on personality theory out of my bookshelf and handed it to Sid. "It's my subject," I said, "I'm crazy." This is my life, an open book.

"I know this book," Sid said, "It's a good intro." He said he'd be very grateful if I would read his dissertation, promised to bring me a copy tomorrow and looked forward to my comments. "You can be *my* coach."

"But tonight," he said, "I just want to go out for a few drinks somewhere and forget *everything*. Someplace different."

A discussion ensued about the taverns on High Street across from campus. There were so many.

"Let's count them," Sid suggested, "One small drink in each place and see how far we get."

"We'll take a survey!" I said, getting enthusiastic, "A small drink could be the house scotch, straight-up. We'll rate them on quality, price, and ambiance!"

"Let's do it!" Sid said, rising to his feet with two thumbs up.

We thoroughly emptied our bladders and put on our jackets. I put a small notebook and pen in the inside pocket of mine. We had a spark in our steps as we walked down Northwood to High Street.

Our first stop was a working-class bar just north of campus. There were plenty of people, but not much activity or noise. 'Old Rockytop' played from the jukebox. There were a couple open stools at the bar, so we bellied up and ordered our scotch. *Highland Mist* was poured and it was cheap, which I commented on. Sid showed me his watch and tapped the face. "Still happy hour," he said, "In fifteen minutes that price will double."

Looking around, I saw it was a *just got off work* crowd, pounding a couple before going home. Then I spotted him at the far

117

end of the bar. It was the guy from group who visualized killing people. I raised my glass to him and nodded.

"Bottoms up!" I toasted Sid, "Let's move on. We have work to do!"

We continued south, visiting two more establishments in the next two blocks. They were both rather quiet, but 'older students' described the clientele. "Civilized," I wrote in my notebook.

Then came the *Symposium Lounge,* which was not as intellectual as it sounds. *Robert Burns* went into our glasses.

The Sports lounge came next and was spic & span with too many lights. There was no music, but a basketball game in progress on some TVs. It felt like we were invading a private club, because everyone was watching us sip our scotch. There were mostly guys in jackets and ties, but also a few girls in skirts with bling. It wasn't exactly prom night, but seemed rather formal for Friday evening at a tavern. "Frat zone," I wrote, "And we do not know the secret handshake."

We were losing our zip and inhibitions by the time we got to Larry's, which had a reputation as a gay hangout. I'd been there before and never saw any overt displays to make me believe that, though I think I'd be comfortable either way. When I was a student, it was distinctly a Hippie bar and I was very comfortable with that.

At the bar we were politely told that spirits are not served at Larry's, just beer and wine. Sid and I looked at each other and shook our heads. Other stops also focused on beer, like the Heidelberg, an emporium for very young people. We were about to leave when we spotted Karl, playing chess at a table with a friend, and we walked over.

"Hey, guys!" Karl greeted, introducing us to his friend. "Have a seat."

We joined them and revealed our mission. I showed Karl my notebook.

"Let me see that," he said, sipping his coffee. He looked over the previous page and laughed, reading aloud, "The Heidelberg: abuse of bodily fluids. This is great! You should have brought your camera, Rick."

A foursome at a corner table punched Elton's "Benny and the jets" on the juke box and were flamboyantly singing along. Whenever the chorus came, they poured it on. "Bu Bu Bu Bu Benny and the Jetssssssssssss," they hissed in each other's faces.

"It's a public place," Karl said, frowning disapproval, "*Anyone* can come here."

Sid and I excused ourselves to continue our quest, feeling a second wind coming on. Andy Capps, a classic English pub, was a comforting discovery: old hardwood bar top and tables, with Cutty Sark in our glasses. We both fell in love with the place and split a plate of fish & chips to fortify us for the next half of campus High Street.

"You know why there are so many bars here?" Sid asked, rhetorically, "It's because there are so many different kinds of people. This just happens to be the one that suits us!"

I took out my notebook and recorded his comments. They were so true.

As we approached 11th avenue and Chittenden, we knew the demographic would change to younger, hornier, and crazier. At the I. P. Lounge, a very drunk girl on the stool next to Sid asked him to buy her a drink, slurring every word. She was probably fresh off the farm, starting university in the big city. Karl was right, I should have brought my camera.

Sid took out a business card from the alcohol abuse clinic where he worked and handed it to her. "Put this in your purse," he said in his therapeutic voice, "I'm a counselor there and my experience tells me you might have a drinking problem." He tried to say more, but she suddenly looked queasy and stumbled quickly to the lady's room.

With yet another scotch under our belts, we walked unsteadily out onto the street and met a pleasant young man leaning against his black Caddy. He engaged us in light conversation and then let us know he had nickel bags of pot for sale. Perhaps our judgment was diminished at that point, but we bought one.

At the southern edge of campus was The Underground, the last stop on our journey. "We made it!" I said, putting my arm around Sid's shoulder, which helped both of us walk straighter.

The underground, as you might imagine, was underground, a large subterranean space, the High Street catacombs. Two bouncers checked I.D.'s on either side of the stairs. I handed mine to one and Sid showed his to the other. They shined their flashlights on them and looked at each other. "You guys are too old for The Underground!" One of them said.

"Way too old," chimed in the other, "There's no one over twenty down there!"

Sid and I started to laugh like we might not be able to stop. Then Sid straightened up, a quick thinker even when drunk. "We're friends of the band," he said slowly. Some pretty good sounds were coming up the stairs. The guardians of the underworld relented and let us pass.

Downstairs, a lot of lovely young girls danced wildly to the music. The live band wailed on Kenny Loggins covers: *I believe in Love*, and then, *Mr. Night*. They nailed us to the wall.

We had a lesson at The Underground about how quickly times change. We had a nickel bag, but no pipe or cigarette papers, so we asked around. No one had papers and we got strange looks. A mere five years before and everyone would have. Between songs, Sid asked the band and one of them gave us a few Zig Zags.

Our tavern crusade was done, but we were a long way from Northwood. We walked the first few blocks north via the alley, so we could roll a small sample. Neither of us had smoked that stuff in a long time. It wasn't very potent.

Near the end of our journey, Northwood felt welcoming. The Boys were sitting on their porch as we approached. We sang "Bu Bu Bu Benny and the Jetsssssss," hissing at them. It was their new house that Art was buying.

We swayed a little on our feet and told them about our tavern survey. They invited us inside, where we met a new face, prettier than The Boys. Wayne introduced us to Elaine, an art history major at the university.

"This house is larger than the rental," Art explained, "So Elaine has the fourth bedroom."

"*Elaine* is one of The Boys?" Sid asked, grinning.

"The Boys?" Elaine asked looking around at all of us, "What?"

"It's what we call these guys," Sid said.

"I was one of The Boys for a while," I added.

"But you *are* a boy," Elaine said.

"Say!" I thought out loud, "Is this a commune, now?"

"These people are all my good friends," Art said, attempting to clarify the situation.

"Yes, a commune," I said, "Just as I suspected."

"I'm obviously not one of *The Boys*," Elaine said, crossing her arms, "You'll need a new epithet for us."

"Hmmm," Sid mused, "Art House pops into my head."

"Art House," Wayne repeated, "I like it."

Elaine

Friday night looked a little fuzzy Saturday morning, but not so much that I couldn't remember the new face at The Boy's house and the fact that I'd seen it before. On a city bus, a few weeks earlier, I was studying people: their expression, how they stood or sat, and their clothing. The interesting ones were targets with my pocket-sized automatic camera, secretly shooting from the hip. No one can hear a shutter on a noisy bus.

Elaine was sitting with her head at an unusual tilt. Her hands together in her lap blended with her arms in a semicircle, framing her upper body and face. It was something like a meditation pose, with a serene air upon her face. I quickly pulled the camera up and down from my trouser pocket and clicked the shutter, hoping to capture her.

Sipping my coffee, I went through my proof sheets on the trunk until I found it. At the time, I was making a series of stylized, silk-screen portraits and thought Elaine might make a good one. I put a fresh piece of paper on my easel and drew her outline from the tiny photograph. Then I got out watercolors and gave it a stenciled look.

When I'm working on a project, I'm pretty focused. Someone quietly walked up the stairs without my notice. I looked away from my work and was startled to see Elaine standing in the doorway of my front room twirling my hat in her hand. She tossed it on the trunk.

"You forgot it when you and your friend returned from La-La Land, last night," she had a whimsically sarcastic way of talking. "*The Boys* thought I should bring it over so I could see *The Loft*.

They said it was different and I see what they meant. If we ever have a parade down Northwood, you'll have the best seat."

"But we do," I said, cleaning my brushes, "every day."

That got a smile out of her. "You're a people watcher, aren't you?" she asked. Then she paused a long moment. "I think you saw me on a bus, recently."

"Well, yeah," I admitted, hoping I wasn't blushing, or that she didn't notice I took her photograph, or that she wouldn't see herself in the painting on my easel. And, oh my God, my proof sheets were on the trunk! I gathered them up and put them away. "What was there about me that made you pick me out?" I asked?

"The wild look in your eyes," she said, "I thought you might be crazy."

"I am," I said, and then quickly added, "but harmless, my psychologist assures me."

Then she even laughed. No longer distracted by my window views, she looked around the room and saw drawings, photographs, prints, and the black ceiling with Big Dipper, Orion, and Cassiopeia. "Oh, my goodness," she said, slapping a hand to her forehead, "You're my father!"

"Huh!" I asked, off balance from the outburst, "Say again?"

"My dad's an artist," she said, "Our house is like a studio." Elaine's dad was indeed a fine artist who worked at a museum, designing exhibit spaces.

"Hello pussycat!" Bagheera entered the room grandly, stretching after a nap. Elaine picked her up and cradled her in her arms. She carried the cat over to my easel. "Something familiar about this," she said, but I could tell she didn't see herself. It wasn't a realistic rendering. "Why didn't you give her hands? Was hand drawing too challenging? Maybe you have an issue with women touching you."

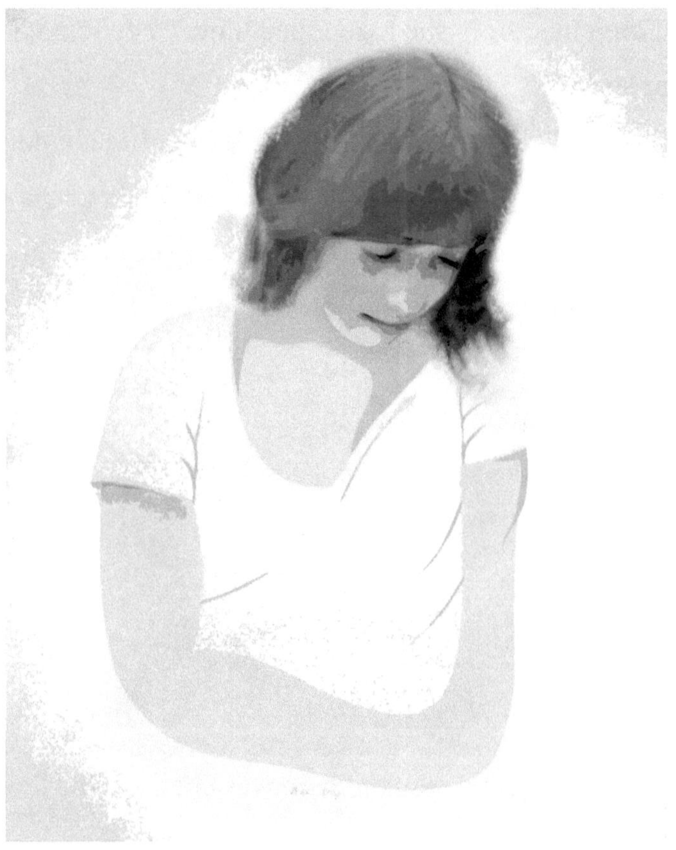

"Feel free to test that theory out." Now, I was laughing. "I already have a shrink," I said. My own analytical wheels started to turn. "If your major was art, per se, you'd be competing with your old man," I suggested, "So art history is the closest substitute."

That time she looked a bit annoyed. "Alright," she said, "We just met, but you scored on that one."

"I'm sorry," I said, "That was group therapy spilling over into everything else."

"Group therapy?" she asked, laughing, "You're not kidding about your shrink?"

"Best thing I ever got into. And it's true, I really don't know you, but they've got some great entry level drawing classes over there and you'll have electives to fill," I said, "They do a good job of making it fun, not intimidating. You wouldn't be better or worse than Dad, just different."

"Yeah, I plan on taking some hands-on art, too," she set Bagheera down on the sofa and spoke to her softly, "He sounds like my father, too."

Mr. Magoo

At the next group session there was another new fool and I knew him, too.

"Mack!" I said, "I *knew* you were crazy!"

"Not again!" Howard said.

"It's alright," I said. "Mack and I are pals. Unless, that is, the group objects." After another thought, I added, "or if Mack objects."

Everyone approved, except George, who said it should be on a trial basis. We welcomed Mack and made introductions around. When we settled down, I asked Mack what brought him to counseling in the beginning.

"A lot of things, really," he began, "I have low feelings of self-worth, but my old man told me every day I wouldn't amount to anything. He'd say that after slapping me around."

Everyone nodded, including George.

"He called me Mr. Magoo," Mack said, pointing to his thick lenses. "I was clumsy, still am, because of my eyes."

Commiserating comments arose around the circle. When it came back to Mack, he leaned forward and looked at the floor, sighing.

"Those are life-long things and you get used to that stuff", he said. "But then I accidentally killed a guy and I can't easily put that behind me."

A few years before, Mack worked for a sign company downtown, doing oil lettering. The erection crew was short-handed one day and he was shanghaied to assist on a repair job with the bucket lift truck.

"When we got there, the erection guy told me I would be operating the lift from below, with him in the bucket," Mack explained. "I strongly objected. He showed me the controls and said it was easy, but it wasn't! I said I couldn't even see up there and we argued, but he insisted." Mack tried his best, but lost control and pushed the bucket into high voltage wires and his co-worker was electrocuted. His story stunned me; *but for the grace of God.*

Mack was silent for a while on the sofa, composing himself. Martha handed him a tissue box. When he continued his story, the rest of us sat in rapt attention.

The police, ambulance, and television cameras came quickly and a major commotion followed. Several eye-witnesses told of Mack arguing against controlling the lift.

"The guy bullied me into it," Mack said, "But how can I be angry with him? He's dead and I killed him."

In the end, Mack was exonerated from all wrong doing by everyone involved, except himself. "If I were stronger willed, I would have refused," he said.

Everyone in the group expressed compassion and support. George spoke for us all, "We're here to help each other."

Wildman!

My reputation on Northwood and beyond was *mild mannered.* I was quiet, reserved, thoughtful, and probably considered a bit crazy, too. But some of us taciturn types show another side when we're sure we're alone. One Saturday morning, I was cleaning up The Loft in a very good mood. I did dishes, sweeping, and tidying, all the while singing loudly along with Phoebe Snow on the stereo. I think I was happy. I picked up

Bagheera and danced flamboyantly around my rooms. Then I saw Arthur standing on my porch roof, watching me through the window.

My music and singing were so loud, I didn't hear him pounding on the front door. Art climbed the tree and stepped off onto the roof, witnessing another me. He climbed through the window into my kitchen.

"I knew there was a Wildman inside you," he laughed, "Why don't you let him out more often?"

Embarrassed, I went into the front room and turned down the stereo so we could hear each other. Art had stopped in to tell me there was going to be an informal gathering at The Boys house that evening.

"No special occasion," he said.

"But we'll make it one, I'm sure," I said

"Bring the Wildman," Art said, going down the stairs, "That would do it."

A get together was just what I wanted. That week at work, I screen-printed T-shirts for some company's staff and there were a couple dozen blank shirts of various sizes left over. I asked Ray, and he said I could have them. After hours, I printed 'I Love Northwood' on them in a fancy script. The party at The Boys house would be my opportunity to give them to everyone.

That evening I deliberately walked down the street late, so everybody would already be there. They got quiet when I came in, wondering what was in the big box. I set it down, opened it up, and passed them out according to sizes. To say they were well received would be an understatement.

"Great!" Wayne said, "We should wear these to the softball game on Saturday!"

Sid sat down with his guitar and spontaneously started composing a song called 'I Love Northwood', sort of a talking blues thing.

As the evening progressed, I noticed Wayne talking a lot more than usual and realized there was no tobacco in his mouth.

"I quit," he said, when I asked. "I got an abscess in my cheek that took a whole lot of time and treatment to get rid of. It scared the hell out of me!"

After a while Art brought out his tempera colors and we started painting each others' faces. I don't know when this started or who thought of it, but it was a regular activity. It seemed to put an exclamation point on the tribal community this neighborhood had become.

I painted cat-like nose and whiskers on Elaine. "You were right about the drawing class," she said, "It was a lot of fun." I cleaned the brush while she looked at herself in a hand mirror, meowing with a smile. "I'm going to take one of the painting courses next quarter. Print-making looks pretty interesting, too."

"I see," I said, "Will I hear that you're switching majors in a few months?"

The smile vanished and she curled her painted fingernails at me like claws. "Give me that brush!" she said, "It's my turn." She dipped deeply in red tempera. "And I'm going to make you look like the devil!"

Walls

In a world that worships money, most everyone I knew had other reasons for living. Wayne's love of animals and benevolent nature led him to Veterinary school. Sid studied Psychology because the human mind fascinated him. Arthur had Frank Lloyd Wright visions with his architecture. Karl was a perfect fit for his job at the photo store.

Making artistic things with my hands was the reason I got up in the morning. *Starving* is the word we associate with artist. Most of the time, it was beauty I sought. Other days, I looked for meaning in my art, images that said something poignant or narrative. That's where my mind was one Saturday morning, before dawn, as I descended from The Loft and stepped out onto Northwood with my camera bag.

"Good morning, Rick!" Carly greeted me from high above, "What are you doing up so early?" She was leaning out her attic window with a cigarette in hand.

"Shhh," I said, holding a finger to my lips, "You'll wake everybody."

"C'mon up," she said, more quietly, "The door's unlocked."

I climbed her many stairs and stopped short on the second floor landing. Through the doorway, I saw a bed had been slept in. There was a teacup on the nightstand and a chewed up bone on the rug. I took the last flight two at a time and flopped on the mattress at her feet. "I'm off on a photographic adventure," I said, catching my breath. Vishnu padded over and flopped on top of me. I put my arm around his neck. "You *look* like a bad-ass watchdog, but we know you're really a big baby." I saw and smelled that Carly's cigarette was marijuana, which she handed me. No generation gap here.

"Oh, Carly," I complained with my voice, but lay on my back and took a deep drag on it, before handing it back. Outside of picture taking, I had no volition.

"You said it was an *adventure,*" she giggled, "And that you were *off."* She poured a mug of tea and handed it to me. "Tell me, Rick," Carly asked, "What do you miss about Cleveland?"

"Well, the lake, of course," I said without hesitation, "I feel kinda land-locked without a beach." I stopped looking at her ceiling and sat up. "I miss the art museum."

"Yeah," Carly said, "and the orchestra. Severance Hall is such a wonderful place."

"I haven't been there in years," I said, "but when I was a kid, we had season tickets every year, front row of the mezzanine."

"That sounds great," she said.

"I used to think about jumping, actually," I said, "But then I'd get lost in the music."

Carly laughed at my childhood craziness. Then she asked me what I was looking to photograph.

"I have no idea," I said, "That's the *adventure* of it, sort of a spontaneous thing. You and Vishnu want to roam the alleyways with me?"

"Got stuff to do today," she said, "but thanks."

Light began to grow in the sky. I finished my tea, moved Vishnu, and started to get up. "You take good care of Carly, today," I said to the dog with one last head scratch.

"Let your path guide you," Carly said, with her wide smile, "Love you, neighbor."

"Love *you*," I said, giving her big toe a little squeeze, before walking down the stairs. I thought about how honest and open Carly was with her feelings. She disarmed me, but if I became Mr. Rogers with everyone, I'd feel vulnerable. But maybe I could bare my soul with art. I wanted to believe that.

Back on the sidewalk, it felt like my day had changed in some important way and tried to put my finger on it. I continued slowly down the nearest alley, which was way more interesting than the street with its mown lawns and trimmed bushes. Alleys have weeds, trash cans, and remnants of the past slowly crumbling with the passage of time.

And it was beautiful, that was the change. My enthusiasm and hunger for making dazzling images was replaced with the wonder and appreciation of how beautiful every little thing was.

It should be noted that digital photography had yet to be imagined. There was a roll of black and white film in my single-lens reflex camera, with 36 frames to shoot. There was more film in my bag, along with a variety of lenses and filters, but I didn't expect to make more than 36 negatives. That meant there wasn't anything random about my photographs. Each shot was taken after a whole lot of looking through the viewfinder from different angles.

The subjects I found myself shooting were walls; brick walls and stone walls made from varying materials. My focusing on them might be symbolic of something on my mind, I thought. Then there were hundred year old walls that were cracked or falling. Were they symbolic for me, I wondered?

A couple hours and a lot of alleys later, I realized I was full of tea, and noticed I was near Ted's apartment. Ted was now my ex-bro in law and good friend. I often joked that I wanted him in the separation agreement. He was a much better brother than the one I was born with. Ted lived with Rita, who I knew from my first days on Northwood, when she was a momentary conquest of Sid's. She was briefly drawn to and then disgusted with his lifestyle. I was pretty sure she would find more stability with Ted.

I knocked on the door and Ted welcomed me in. He didn't look too chipper that morning.

"My primary goal in visiting," I confessed, "Is to use your bathroom." Rita was washing her hair in the kitchen sink as I made my way to the necessary. When I came out, she sat on a chair, drying her hair. I sat in another, facing her. "Morning, Rita," I said, "How are you?"

She stopped drying and let the towel drape across her head. She had a stoic look and, with the towel, reminded me of so many portraits of Saint Mary. "May I photograph you?" I asked.

"Sure," she said, without emotion.

I carefully focused and took a shot. Then I repositioned myself and took another, the last two frames on my roll of film. "That's great," I said.

"What are you seeing?" she asked.

"With that towel and your expression, I'm seeing the Madonna," I said, "With a child in your arms it would be perfect."

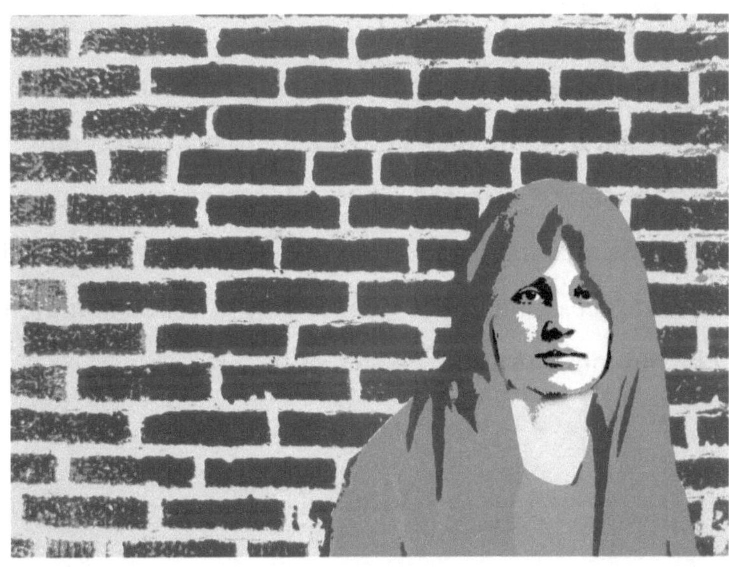

Rita pulled the towel over her face. Ted came in and stood behind her chair, putting his hands lovingly on her shoulders.

135

"Did I say something wrong?" I asked.

Rita took the towel off and straightened up, keeping the serious look. "We just got home," she said, "I had an abortion, this morning."

"Oh, my God!" I said, "I'm so sorry."

"It's alright," she said, "You didn't know."

Could I have intuited it, I wondered, thinking about Carly's mystical ways. "Still, I'm so sorry," I repeated, more softly, "That can't be easy."

"I haven't ruled out motherhood for the future," Rita said, "Just for now."

I walked home more directly, with a quick step. After a brief conversation with Bagheera, I got out my chemicals. Under the darkness of a thick blanket, I loaded my film on a reel and put it in the tank. An hour later I was examining my finished negatives with a magnifying glass where they hung to dry in my bathroom.

A week later I prepared photo silk-screens and made an edition of prints, placing Rita in front of one of my walls. I called it, *Madonna and Bricks;* an image I hoped would say something that couldn't be put into words.

Mack

Mack and I left the sign shop for lunch one Friday and went to Oldfield's, a bar and grill nearby. The idea was a burger and a beer, but Mack surprised me by having a couple serious drinks while we waited for our food.

Back at the shop, Ray could see Mack was unsteady. I only had beer on my breath, but that was just as bad to Ray. He said our workday was over and to never come in the shop like that again. He wasn't angry and sounded more like my dad giving me advice. I was embarrassed and swore there wouldn't be a second time.

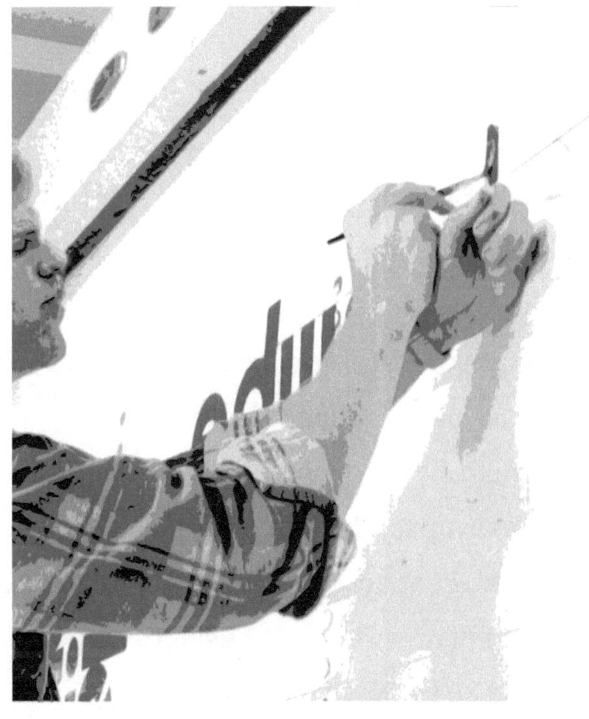

Mack did it again a month later and then a third time. "I'm sorry Mack, but that's strike three," Ray said. "You're a good sign painter, but I can't have that. Pack up your brushes and go. I'll send you your last paycheck." That time, too, he wasn't angry. He looked very sad and spoke softly.

Mack didn't seem to mind being fired. "You're right, Ray," he said, "I'd get rid of me, too, if I were you."

A few weeks later, I saw him at Dick's. He was pretty wasted that night, too. I asked why he stopped going to group therapy, but a shrug was the only answer I got. He hadn't found another job, but said some freelance work came his way. Then I didn't see him for a long time.

As spring approached, I ran into him one night on High Street. He looked terrible and had a bad cough. "What is going on with you?" I probed. He didn't want to tell me, but I got it out of him. He got evicted from his apartment and was living in an unheated garage he rented for storage. "My friend," I said in disbelief, "That's one step away from homeless!" We were still getting frosts, and the garage sounded insane.

I invited him to sleep on my sofa for a while, until he got his life together. He came up to The Loft and I pointed to the shower. While he was in there, I got out some clean clothes and tossed his in my laundry. Then I put on some chicken soup and took an inventory of my cold and flu medications.

After a week, Mack's health returned, but not much else. There didn't seem to be any light in his eyes. During the time I knew him, his life was in steady decline. He wasn't looking very hard for a job. In fact, he wasn't doing much of anything.

The season turned and it was warmer outside. I asked him to move on. "You're a good friend, Rick," Mack said, "I would have thrown me out long before this."

I was relieved to have my space back, but sick at heart. Self-discovery doesn't come to everyone.

Any Excuse for a Party

The day opened quietly, then quickly evolved into much ado about nothing. That's how we did things on Northwood.

The sun rose above the trees in a clear sky, shining down our street where I walked to Sid's house, finding him on the porch with coffee and paper. I was returning his dissertation about religiosity and a couple pages of notes I made. He welcomed me and offered coffee, then eagerly looked over my notes.

His paper thoroughly passed my inspection, except for several typos I knew he'd be happy I found. One section confused me a bit, so I reworded the introduction for clarity. Maybe he would agree. Then there was one other thing on my mind.

"I liked your study," I said, "But I'm a little surprised by what you didn't include."

"Oh, yeah?" he asked. "Not comprehensive? I thought I beat the subject to death."

"Well, you talk a lot about surrender," I started, "for better or worse, and the relationship between anxiety and religion, which was great. But I'm surprised you didn't investigate religiosity and *sexuality*, especially vis a vis surrender."

"I'll be damned," Sid said, "That didn't occur to me, but I see what you're saying."

"Maybe too close to home," I suggested. "I probably saw that because of Tess and the guru. She is, in fact, at some kind of guru retreat this weekend. I have a personal problem with surrender, maybe from being held down a lot as a kid. Tess does this thing where she draws on my chest with her finger and I surrender because it's adorable. But after a dozen times, I realized she was writing her name across my chest! Now I feel funny about it."

"Thanks for doing this," he held up my notes, "But you remind me of something I have to tell you." He leaned to me and spoke more softly. "I've been seeing the same woman for a month, avoiding all others."

"Oh, my God!" I said, startled, spilling some coffee on my pants, "Is this the dawning of a new era?"

"Maybe. I wanted to try a less complicated lifestyle for a while," Sid said, "And she's a sweetheart."

As I tried to absorb this monumental news, a stranger came out of The Boy's former abode and walked our way. He looked to be several years older than me, heavy set with an irregular gate. He came up to Sid's porch to introduce himself.

He was Greg, a lawyer who was starting an independent law practice out of the house. For the last several years, he was an assistant Ohio attorney general. "Don't be impressed," he said with a disarming smile, "There are lots of assistants. They take all the silly, stupid cases that the attorney general doesn't want to be bothered with. Pretty boring job, really"

Next it was Wayne joining us, whom Greg already met. The *Arthouse* concept didn't stick, and the new place was still The Boy's house, which Elaine took with good humor.

"Hey," Wayne asked, "Did you guys know that Arthur is leaving next week?" None of us did. "He's studying in England for a semester. I thought a small 'going away' picnic might be in order."

It was a tiny seed that was just introduced to fertile soil. Sid suggested it could be a surprise party. Being into signs, I thought a 'goodbye' banner stretching across the street would surprise the pants off him.

Karl came downstairs and out the door, coffee mug in hand, as always. "I'm hearing plotting and scheming from above," he said, grinning, "What's going on?"

We introduced him to Greg and filled him in. Karl liked the banner idea and asked Greg if he'd mind hanging one with a rope from his upstairs window to Karl's.

"Sounds like fun," Greg said. He looked a tad bewildered by the party snowball effect. "This is going to be an event, isn't it?" he asked me.

"Welcome to Northwood," I said.

The Event

The small seed morphed into a virus spreading down the street. Sid called his brother, Dan, infecting his neighborhood as well. Wayne and I thought a keg was a good idea, seeing the size of this *small picnic* get out of control. We walked down the street to get his car, stopping at his house to give Max and Elaine an update.

Fitz arrived while we were there, a man I disliked the minute I met him. He was a dope peddler who made house calls. Max contacted him for a bag of pot. The minute Elaine left the room, he started bragging about all the women he was screwing, using very vulgar language. "Women *say* they want a sensitive man," he said, "But what they really want is a barbarian!" The man looked barbaric, too; burly and hairy, the missing link. Max, unfortunately, invited him to the party. Then Fitz started talking about the beautiful, big breasted woman he'd bring. He boasted he'd been 'putting it to her' anytime he wanted, all week.

"Let's get out of here," I said to Wayne.

"A barbarian, indeed," Wayne said in the car.

"I'm with you," I said, "What a jerk!"

A keg is very heavy, even for two healthy young men. We muscled it into the trunk and drove to the veterinary school, where we rolled it across the operating room and into the cadaver cooler. It had an air of chemicals and small body bags with a tag on each one. On our way out, I checked out all the fancy gadgetry around the operation tables.

Wayne picked up a mask connected to a tank. "Want to really relax?" he asked. The tank was labeled Nitrous Oxide.

"No, thanks," I said, "Not that relaxed."

Around noon, I met up with Sid at The Loft to work on the banner. In the spirit of blowing things out of proportion, I decided to make a portrait of Arthur in the center. I cut an old sheet in half and got Sid started on the lettering. In my trunk, I sifted through my photo history until I found a few I made of Arthur for his passport, reflecting on how long ago that seemed. What will it feel like, I wondered, when I look into this trunk of relics in forty years? Maybe I'll write a book about them.

Les wandered up to see what was going on. He picked up one of my brushes and gave Sid a hand. As we worked, I asked them if they had met a pot dealer named Fitz.

"Regrettably," Sid said.

"What an asshole," Les added, "I'd never buy his shit."

"Max invited him to the party," I told them.

"Oh, no," Sid said, "Thanks for the warning, Bro."

My portrait turned out to be a decent rendering and Sid and Les made some nice informal lettering. We laid out the pieces and sewed them together.

Greg, who I soon learned was very clever, devised a looped pulley system from his place to Karl's. They were ready to send the banner across the street as soon as we brought it to them. The effect was outrageous.

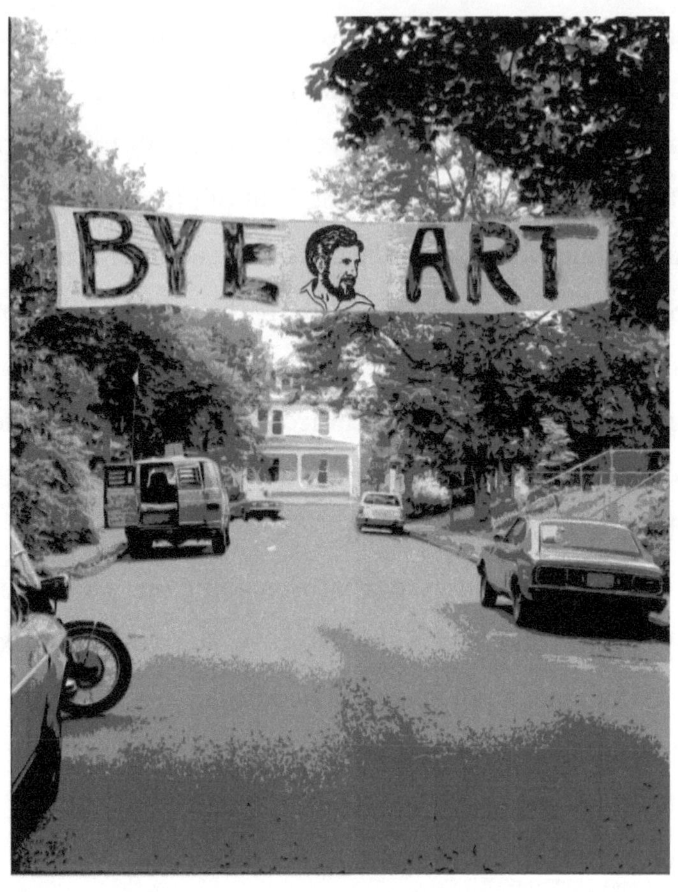

Earlier, Max talked Art into taking him on a manufactured errand on his motorcycle all the way to Upper Arlington, getting him out of the way. Tables were set up, grills were lit, and salads were tossed. Wayne and I retrieved the keg. "No, I still don't want recreational Nitrous, thank you, Wayne." The evening was a bit of a letdown for the principals who dreamed it on Sid's porch that morning. We were too tired to party! It was fun, though, to see Arthur stopping on his bike in front of the banner in shock. "How the hell did this happen?" he asked all the people coming out into the street to greet him.

"Everything to excess!" shouted Sid from his porch.

I sat at a table on the edge of activity with Carly and Vishnu, who was looking restless. We kept him between us, giving him lots of love and comfort. Les and Jill joined us, familiar faces to Vishnu, who began to settle down.

Then I saw her, my ex, with Fitz, by the keg. I was feeling so good up to that point. They were here and there about the party, until he left her to talk to someone across the street. I excused myself from my friends and went to her.

"I thought you were the modern, *liberated* woman," I said to her.

She turned to me. "What are you talking about?" she asked, sounding like I was the last person she wanted to talk to.

"Listen a minute," I sighed, "I'm no longer unhappy and, in fact, I'm grateful that we're not together anymore. But we were sort of family for a long time, so I feel obligated to give you some information."

"I'm listening," she said.

"Fitz," I said, "That Neanderthal you're with. This morning, he was bragging about how he's been using you any way he wants all week. He's the biggest objectifier of women I've ever met. I thought you'd like to know, since you're the modern, independent woman and all."

"Well, thank you," she said. "I can see you have my interests at heart, but you should really let go. My life is none of your business." She turned and walked away.

So what? It was a long day. I walked back to The Loft and watched the party for a while from my windows. Bagheera rubbed against my legs, purring. I picked her up and lay down on the sofa, petting her. Tomorrow would be a day of rest, I promised myself.

Greg

Greg did a lot of walking. If he needed to go far, there was a bus stop about a block away. On my way home from work, I saw him several blocks from home with a bag of groceries, so I stopped and offered him a ride. He put his bag on the back seat and got in the front, thanking me. I was on foot when I first got to Northwood and hadn't forgotten the hassles.

The reason Greg didn't have a car, he explained, was that he was inept at driving. One eye was nearsighted and the other farsighted, causing him poor depth perception. As a teenager, he longed to drive, but failed driver training and the license test multiple times. "The written part is a breeze, but I can't drive," he said, "I kept scraping against guardrails and parked cars, so I gave up the idea."

Greg was uncoordinated in many ways. He was the kid who would rather read a book than play baseball. Other kids made fun of him when he tried. Intellectual pursuits came easily though, being exceptionally gifted.

I mentioned that I lived with The Boys in his house for a while, and he invited me in to see what he'd done with it. I carried his groceries up the front steps. "I haven't met my next door neighbor yet," Greg said, finding his keys, "Someone told me she lives in the attic!"

"Carly's alright," I said, "just a little unusual. But I think she's starting to come downstairs lately."

Greg's front room was neat and clean, but lacking in decorative charm. The hardwood floor looked like it experienced sanding and varnish since I saw it last. The dartboard wall was smoothed out and painted. I was partly responsible for its previous condition. "I haven't done much in here, yet," Greg said, "The office was the priority."

The downstairs bedroom Arthur used to occupy was transformed into a first-class law office: a nice big desk surrounded by hardwood bookcases filled with musty old legal volumes. Greg sat down behind the desk. The environment fit him perfectly. "I'm afraid your case is hopeless," he intoned like Perry Mason, pointing at me, "The judge will show you no mercy."

Cats!

On Saturday morning, Greg called me to ask if I might walk across the street and witness the signing of a legal document. It wasn't raining or anything, so I didn't mind. Greg was finishing up with his clients, a young couple, and only needed to ink some papers. It felt a little uncomfortable, because they were all dressed very nicely, while I sat down, unshaven, in my paint-splattered cut-off jeans and bedroom slippers. I didn't know I'd be called upon to bear witness. The couple hurried out as soon as pens were laid to rest.

I lingered in my chair. "Is this going to be a regular thing?" I asked.

Greg smiled. "Many legal documents require a third-party witness. Is that alright?"

"Will these be *come as you are* parties?"

Greg laughed. "I like that part," he said, "It breaks the tension."

I started to get up, when Greg said, "Your lights go off and on a lot, late at night. I have a fantasy that you're a mad scientist, experimenting in your laboratory by the light of the moon." He said it like Boris Karloff might have.

"Sort of," I said, "You got the *mad* part right. If you don't have another client for a while, why don't you come up to The Loft?"

He followed me out the door, repeating with raised eyebrows, "The Loft!"

"Nice!" he said taking in my windowed room, like everybody did, "What a view! You'd never guess it was like this from the street."

I showed him the darkroom/art studio/domicile set up and pointed out some of my art projects.

"Projects!" he repeated, "I love it!" Looking around my darkroom/bedroom, he saw my tape recorder by my pillow. "What's that about?"

"That's my dream project," I said. I explained about recording dreams without moving the head. My theories about the nature of dream imagery and communication particularly interested him.

"You're full of *projects,*" he said, excitedly, "You *are* a mad scientist! This is how Franklin found electricity and Edison made the light bulb!"

"Well, I don't know about that," I said, "I don't think any of my ventures are of a practical nature, they're just about discovering who I am. I haven't formulated a grand unification theory in physics or anything."

We drifted back into the front room where Greg was startled by Bagheera on the arm of the sofa next to him. He flinched and stepped away. Poor Greg had gone through childhood without ever experiencing a pet. I picked up Bagheera and gently introduced the two of them. He very tentatively put out his hand to pet her head as he saw I was doing, and Bagheera batted at it, claws retracted. Greg laughed with childlike abandon.

I had a length of yarn tied to a little wooden spool, which I pulled around the floor. Bagheera chased and pounced on it. "That's instinctive hunting behavior, isn't it?" Greg asked. I handed the yarn to him, and for a long time he moved around the room laughing and playing with Bagheera.

"I can't believe this!" he laughed, "I love cats and I didn't know it!"

Running

Sid's *steady* girlfriend, Jenny, was into running and way healthy for doing so. Sid started running with her and his extra weight disappeared fast. Elaine and The Boys were inspired by them and began jogging, too. Looking down from The Loft, I saw healthy looking neighbors running by regularly. Some recent health issues made me think a change in lifestyle was in my future as well. Getting decent shoes was the first step.

I didn't share this thought with anyone. The truth is that I wasn't sure I *could* run. The anonymity of running in the dark appealed to me, so about ten, one night, I laced up my new cross-trainers and had at it.

I knew I wasn't ready for an uphill course, so I ran along the side street to Northwood which was mostly level. After about four blocks, I slowed to a stop and almost barfed. But I walked around for a few minutes and was able to run back. This wasn't going to be easy, but I was in such bad shape, something had to be done. Each night, I made it a bit farther, feeling less terrible.

A week or so later, I was jogging along with the ten thousand thoughts, when I noticed the landscape was unfamiliar. I turned and ran downhill to High Street, were I could see where I was. I had run almost two miles and wasn't particularly tired! I ran along High to Northwood and uphill to The Loft. It felt great! Then, like everyone else, I became a running evangelist.

Greg called me Saturday morning and asked if I could come over. There were no clients or papers to sign. Greg had a cat in his arms. He wanted advice about a few cat things, looking a bit nervous and agitated.

"This is Angel," he introduced us, "I thought I was prepared for this, but I found a flea this morning! She's scratching up my furniture, too."

"And if you only want one cat," I warned, "You need to have her spayed soon."

We sat down and discussed vets, flea control options, scratching posts, types of food, and catnip. I reminded him that Wayne was studying to become a veterinarian and could be counted on for good advice.

"Getting Angel is a little more involved than I thought," he said, "Thanks for helping." Finally, he noticed I wasn't my usual

Saturday morning disheveled self, taking in my new shoes and athletic attire. "Oh, no!" he said, "Not you, too!"

I described my progress and how healthy I felt. "Why don't you try it with me?" I urged. "I'm hoping to do the next Dick's Den Marathon!"

"Are you kidding me?" he asked, "I don't even walk very well!"

"Listen, man," I said, "If I can get into this, anyone can. It's way easier than driving!"

What's in a name?

The sign shop job was not my first experience with the industry in Columbus. After dropping out of Ohio State, I was only twenty years old, couldn't find a steady job immediately, and worked a dozen temp jobs for an agency near campus. The last one was with a large sign business downtown. They had a hand-lettering department, a photo silk screen operation, an exhibit building crew, and a room with flexographic printing presses which made custom labels.

The label room was windowless and just large enough for the four presses and about a hundred gallon jugs of ink, most of them less than half full and randomly distributed around the floor and various shelves. The three pressmen who worked there were too busy filling orders to address the ink mess, so I was hired for the day to consolidate inks of the same color and arrange them alphabetically.

That didn't take very long and I wanted a full day of work, so I cleaned the jugs with thinner and made new, easy to read, labels for them all. Then I cleaned the room itself, all around the presses from floor to ceiling. The pressmen were very happy about that.

There were still a couple hours in the work day and management hadn't even checked on my progress, so I looked around for something else to do. The pressroom was heavy with toxic ink and thinner odor. An exhaust fan high on the wall in one corner blew air out and an intake vent was near the floor opposite. My remembrance of high school chemistry made me think these particular odors, all petroleum distillates, were heavier than ordinary fresh air. I explained and asked the guys if they'd mind if I tried something different.

I saw that the exhaust fan was only a plug in, so I found a step ladder and some tools to remove it. Then I cleaned it, oiled the moving parts, and installed it blowing out at the intake vent below. When I turned it on, there was almost immediate relief, fresh air poured in from above. The press guys looked at me in amazement. The manager came in shortly after and looked around at the clean and tidy room. The press men told him this kid was awesome and should be hired. They pointed out that the fourth printing press was idle and they could teach me to operate it. It was a smaller press than the others, designed for short runs of smaller labels. I was hired full time, but only minimum wage to start, two dollars an hour at the time.

A week later I was cranking out label orders and getting a lot of positive feedback from the guys. I was also getting acquainted with the entire business. The silk screen coordinator interested me, because he was mostly in the darkroom, a familiar environment. He was considered very clever and called *The Wizard* by his co-workers. I'd never worked with the graphic arts film he made screens with and asked a lot of questions. He was happy to invite me in and give me a tutorial about it.

My third week there, I caught them up on the small run label orders for my press, and The Wizard asked management if he could have me in screen printing for a while. That week I learned the basics of his operation.

When my thirty day *probation period* was over, the manager told me I would get ten cents an hour raise. I was stunned, but young and inexperienced, so I asked The Wizard, who told me everyone in his area made more than twice my wage and I should demand more. But I felt so insulted, knowing I'd done great work, I quit right then, middle of the day, punched my card out and went home to my apartment. They had my number and could call if they wanted me. They didn't. Welcome to the working world. But I started writing about this experience for an entirely different reason.

The hand lettering crew at that first job were the most artistically talented people in the place, so I observed them in action whenever I had the opportunity. They were a temperamental group, too, but the friendliest ones were not annoyed by my questions and explained some of their technique. It fascinated me to learn that they considered themselves craftsmen, not artists. I was corrected when I used the word artist.

One sign painter, only a few years my senior, interested me more than the others, because he came to work in a suit and tie! He removed the jacket, parked it on a fancy wooden hanger, strapped a spotless apron on himself, and got to work. He was *absolutely* an artist, very accurate and quick with his brushes.

I visited him several times at his easel, and I could tell he enjoyed my company and questions. His name was Diego, and had a Spanish, not Mexican, air. Along with being nattily attired, he was perfectly groomed, every hair in place with a tidy little *pencil* mustache. He used Spanish words for some things, and called me Rico after I introduced myself. His dramatic flair and absence of a clear accent gave me the slight suspicion that the Spanish thing might be a put-on. There was a bit of rogue about him.

I commented on his fastidious appearance and he carefully put his brush and pallet down to address me with his full attention. "Do you do neat, careful work?" he asked.

"I think so," I said, "It's surely my intention."

"Then why don't you dress that way?" he asked, tapping the back of his hand on my chest. "Did you get that shirt at the Salvation Army?" He was emphatic.

"Well," I started, but couldn't find the words. I did, in fact, buy *all* my clothes at the thrift store. It was what I could afford.

"My life's work is about neatness," he explained, "And *everything* in my life must be equally neat and in order. They overlap and carry over into each other!" He sighed and put a hand to his forehead, searching for the right words. "The clothes make the man!" he exclaimed! "It's not just a cliché. If you want to be a professional, you've got to look and feel like a professional." His words and philosophy stuck with me after I moved on, and I tried to adopt some of that attitude, though interpreted in my own way.

Five years later, when I *was* the professional photo silk screen guy, I came to work one morning and was surprised to find Diego, the immaculate perception, putting on his apron. The moment he saw me, he put a finger to his lips, looking serious. Ray motioned me over and introduced us. "I'd like you to meet Manuel," he said, "Manuel, this is Rick, our photo-screen man."

Manuel (Diego?) offered his hand. "A pleasure, Rick," he said in his gentlemanly way, "Would it be alright if I call you Rico?"

When Ray went back to his office and Manuel started lettering his first sign, I wandered over, making sure my back was to Mark. "Are you on the lam, *Diego*?" I asked, quietly, "Or just schizophrenic?"

"None of the above," he said, calmly concentrating on his work.

"It's about a woman, isn't it?" I asked, getting a brief smile, which he put away quickly.

"So, Rico," he said, ignoring my question, "You've come up in the world. Ray says you do good work, but you still look like a bum! You didn't even shave, this morning!"

Tess, trying to listen twenty feet away, stepped toward us to defend me. "Ricky is just being himself like most of our generation," she said, "You're the one who's different!"

"But this *is* who I am," he said to her. Then he turned to me and smiled. "Ricky?" he asked very softly, "Really?"

I turned to go back to my area, but Mark caught my eye, signing, "He's a strange one." We had a short conversation about him, ending with us both chuckling.

"Sign language?" Manuel asked.

"It was the only way to get to know Mark," I said.

"Rico, Rico, Rico," Manuel said, "I take back everything I said about you."

As I left the room, I heard him behind me. "Hey!" he said, "I'm going to like working here!"

Innocence

Tess, Bagheera, and I were in my bed at The Loft on a weeknight trying to get some sleep. Les and his band had a weekend gig coming up and practiced late downstairs. They tried to be considerate, with the amps very low and dampers on the drums, but a low rumble came to us through the floor. Around midnight,

Jill came upstairs in her nightgown and wearily snuggled into bed beside me.

"I can't sleep down there," she said groggily, "and I'm working tomorrow." Then she saw Tess on the other side of me. "Oh, Tess!" she said, rising on her elbow and looking more awake, "I'll sleep on the sofa." She got up. "Is there a blanket out there?"

"Hall closet," I said, "There's another pillow in there, too."

Jill went out into the hall, and then turned around and came right back, holding bedding to her breast. "Rick and I are just friends, Tess," she said, and went out to the sofa.

Tess was up on her elbow, too. In the moonlight, she looked alarmed.

"Just *friends*," I repeated, "That's true."

Tess closed her eyes and rolled over. "I don't have a claim on you," she said.

"Well," I tried to think of something to say, "I mean, Jill, you know?" I paused and tried again. "I'm an innocent bystander here!"

Tess turned and gave me a tiny kiss. "I'm tired." Somehow, we all managed to get some sleep.

As daylight broke too soon, I heard someone knocking on the wall at the bottom of my stairs. Les wouldn't knock, so it had to be someone else. I slipped on my shorts and went to the top of the steps. "Hello?" I called as quietly as I could.

My ex came up the stairs with both arms around a large box. She put it in my arms and I set it down on the kitchen table.

"I cleaned out a closet, yesterday," she said, "And found some stuff I thought you might want."

I glanced through it: a few old clothes of mine, an old blanket, a pair of decaying shoes I only wore for dirty work, and a few other meaningless odds and ends. "Umm..." I mumbled, "Thanks." Talk about rude awakenings.

"I've been missing you so much!" she blurted out.

What the hell? How was I supposed to react to *that*! She sure didn't seem to miss me a year ago. Her life was *none of my business*, as I recalled. If only I were still dreaming.

I had no response, but the toilet flushed, the bathroom door opened, and Jill came out in her lacy nightie with an early morning aura about her.

I introduced my ex with, I think, my thumb and two terse words. Jill immediately grasped the *entire* situation. She sexily wiggled over and put her arms around my neck. "Thank you so much, Rick," she said with a breathy *Marilyn Monroe* voice that dripped sensuality. It was an effort to keep a straight face. She gave me a little kiss and slapped me, playfully. "You need a shave, you big gorilla!" Then she bounced down my steps giggling.

"Love you," I called after her, meaning it.

"Well," my ex said, "I've been worried about you, but..."

That's when Tess came yawning and stretching out of the bedroom, wearing one of my extra-large 'I Love Northwood' T-shirts for a nightgown. Having met the ex before, she gave us both a bit of the Queen Elizabeth wave on her way to the bathroom.

I turned and looked into the eyes of the one I shared *everything* with for several years. "Life goes on," I said, with a casual shrug.

She bid a quiet adieu, walked down the stairs and out of my life. Thank you.

Another flush and Tess came out. I told her about the box, gesturing to the kitchen table. She looked inside and pulled up a rotting shoe, frowning.

"I think," she said, looking a bit more, "that this is a big box of nothing!" She turned and casually started writing her name on my chest with her finger, but I caught her hand in mine and slowly led her back down the hall to the bedroom.

16th Ave. Festival

Tess and I were seeing each other less frequently. Forgetting to take the photo of her guru off my dartboard was a major blunder. She didn't speak to me for a week after that. I didn't want to hurt her feelings, but I loathed the guru. Somehow we got along better then, perhaps because our differences came into sharper focus. We forgot about the future, enjoyed our time together, and fulfilled each other's need in bed occasionally.

On a Sunday morning, after foraging for provisions across the Olentangy, I saw a lot happening in the distance on High Street.

Tess said it was the Sixteenth Avenue Festival, a mix of politics and art that started several years earlier in 1972.

"Lance and Angel have a booth," Tess said, "Let's check it out!"

Rather than going back to The Loft first, we walked to the show with our vegetables, Tess with her large shoulder bag and me with my backpack. Honestly, we did so much walking in those days, it would have been impossible to gain weight. Our hearts were healthy.

There was a big crowd, a band playing on a central stage, and maybe fifty booths. About a third of those were social and political organizations. I stopped at the Columbus Free Press booth. I'm all about alternative media and politics, but these people were stoned *every time* I had any contact with them. Changing the world requires clear thinking once in a while.

We found Lance and Angel halfway up the street. He had a ton of clocks he made out of thin lacquered slices of a cherry tree he needed to cut down in his back yard. They were very nice, with bark around the edges, and selling right and left. I wanted to ask him about this exhibiting thing, but he was too busy to talk.

Lance and Angel were also devotees to this guru from India, but were both born Jewish. At their front door, there was a mezuzah. I kissed my hand and touched it whenever I walked in. They never mixed meat and dairy, making it difficult to order pizza with them. Lance *always* had his head covered, although it wasn't a yarmulke. I could see how Tess's Catholic background translated to guru worship, but Lance and Angel were harder to figure out. I connected with them in every other way.

Tess and I unburdened ourselves of veggies at the back of their booth, to walk the rest of the show. "Been to the Garden of Eden again?" Angel asked, peeking into my pack.

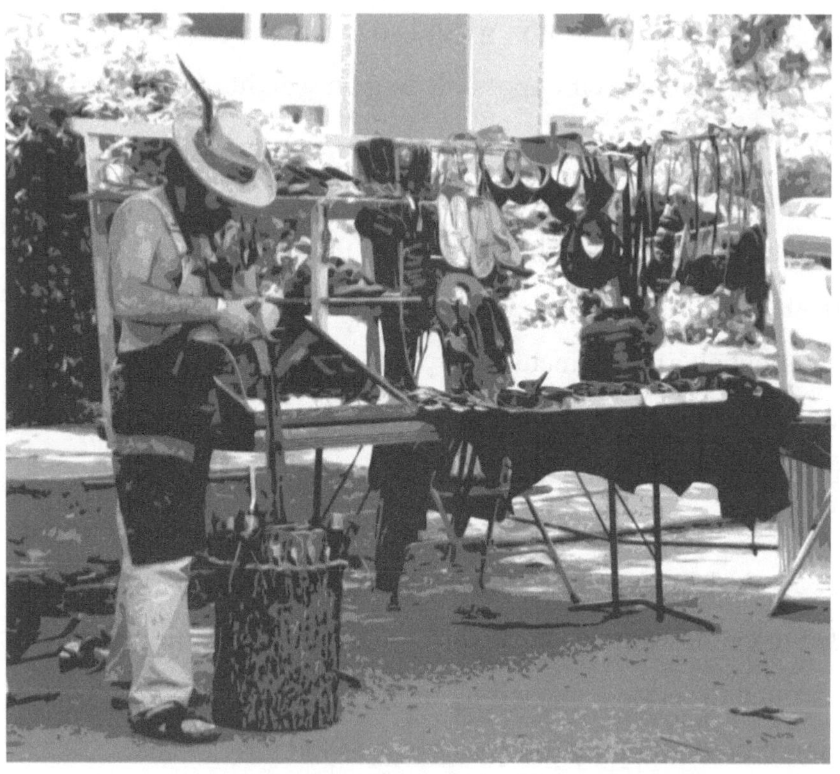

"Plenty to share," Tess said, as we continued up the street.

The shoe repair dude I took my boots to in winter had a booth. He had an array of attractive leather goods: wallets, belts, and handbags, mostly. He also looked like he was doing very well, no time to talk.

"We should try this sometime," Tess said.

"I don't think I have enough stuff for a show like this," I said. Questions and anxieties came to me. Can anyone buy a booth, or do you have to compete for a space? What does it cost? This show is nearby, but a show farther away would require a hotel. It looked complicated.

"Between the two of us, we have a booth full of art," Tess said, "And it might be fun!"

Everything Changes

Buddha said everything changes. Sometimes that's wonderful, and sometimes it kicks you in the pants. Mary McFreud took a counseling job in another city and invited me in for a final session. I confess to feeling a little jolt of panic when I heard the news, but our last visit turned out to be more of a friendly chat than therapy.

My screen-prints and photographs were on my mind, so the conversation started there. I brought a few as a parting gift and went on and on about how I went about making them. "I applied to three art festivals," I said, "And got accepted to all of them!" It was an exciting experiment to see if I could make part of my income with my art.

"I'm so happy for you," she said. When we started these visits, I trembled with anxiety and pain. Now, at the end, I trembled with a positive look at the future. "I think you're done with counseling for a while," Mary said, "And the next time you feel anxiety coming on, it won't be as bad, because you know the questions."

"Questions?" I asked, "You mean like: what am I saying to myself with this anxiety?"

"Exactly so," she said, "and what can I do to bring back my feelings of self value, my okay-ness?"

"But anxiety is likely to return," I asked, solemnly, "Isn't it?"

"By nature and experience, you're very excitable and emotional," she said smiling, "and life brings us a lot of challenges. Self-discovery is a continuing process for all of us."

We said our goodbyes and had a warm hug. I looked around her office one last time, and at *the empty chair*, emptier now than it was a year ago. A few tears came to me as they always had and always would, with very little to induce them. I surrender to that.

Mary walked down the hall with me and I commented that I still hadn't found Miss Right. "But you keep saying you want to be friends with your ideal mate," she said, "Maybe you've already met her, but overlooked the possibility."

Back at The Loft, I lay back on the sofa with Bagheera purring on my chest and a warm breeze coming through my windows. Maybe I *had* met her. I reached for the notebook and pen on my trunk and thought about all the women I'd ever known. Perhaps I could, at least, come up with some qualities I was looking for, like appreciating and respecting each other.

My old schoolmate came to mind and I wrote Lynne. But she was married and, after a minute, I crossed out her name. Then I thought some more and again I wrote Lynne. I was married when I spoke with her on the phone a few years ago. What if she got unmarried? But that was pretty unlikely and she'd probably think it was a crazy idea anyway. I tossed the pad with a single name on it back on my trunk.

"I think Lynne might have been the one," I said to Bagheera, "and I missed my chance a long time ago."

Salesman

Manuel/Diego, or whoever the hell he was, never talked about himself or his past. The only thing we all knew about him, was that he was a very good and very quick sign painter.

One afternoon, he finished a sign and walked over to the bulletin board where work orders for the various areas of the business hung from pushpins. No lettering jobs were posted at the moment. He got out a long paper banner, like we used for grocery store window signs, and pinned it up on his easel. Then he got out his tempera brushes and paints.

I stepped out of the darkroom as he put finishing touches on a faux grocery sign that read: SOAP IS CHEAP!, with colorful bubbles all around it. Mark saw me and signed, "The man is crazy!"

The sign would look great in my stairwell entryway, so I walked over to see if I could have it. Just then, Ray came out of his office and shouted, "What the hell are you doing!"

Manuel pointed to the job board. "There's not enough work for us!" he said.

"That's no reason to waste materials!" Ray replied.

"Alright," Manuel said, "Don't have a heart attack." He took down the banner and handed it to me by the corners. "Here, Rico." I walked it over to a nearby drying rack.

"I'm sorry," Ray said, "I've been too busy with tax forms this week to make sales calls."

"Send *me* on a sales call," Manuel said, "I'd be good at that." He put on his suit coat and straightened his tie, dramatically, to make the point.

I could tell Ray liked this idea. "You do make a good impression," Ray said, "But there's more to estimating a job than that."

"Teach me," Manuel implored. He held out his arms and rotated in a circle.

Ray paced around for a minute, thinking about it. "I've got an appointment to make a bid on some work tomorrow morning," he said. "For starters, why don't you come with me? Come in half an hour early and we'll do some talking."

Good salesmanship, after all, is sort of a con game, and in the next few weeks, Manuel took to it with energy and enthusiasm.

Ray loved it. He didn't really *like* the sales part of the business, preferring to stay in the shop and use his lettering brushes.

Manuel found work for my department, too. He noticed the coin operated newspaper boxes on every street corner had screen printed signs which slipped into slots on the front. Every couple weeks they changed. One would be about sports coverage, then fashion or business news was depicted.

There were two newspapers in Columbus at the time: the evening paper was The Dispatch, which everyone called The *Dogpatch*, and the morning Citizen's Journal, frequently referred to as the Citizen's *Urinal*. Manuel walked cold into both and came away with a six month contract to make the signs for The Dispatch boxes.

He looked very pleased with himself, as he showed me the specs. "You know, Rico," he said, "I might have been mistaken about my true calling."

Roberto

After several months at the sign shop, Manuel didn't come to work one Monday. As the artsy crew was finishing lunch, Ray decided to give him a call. He stood, holding the phone in silence for a minute, then put it down, turning to us. His expression was puzzled. "His phone has been disconnected."

Knowing the guy had a few secrets, I had a hunch he wouldn't be back. "I've been to his place," I said, "I'll check him out after work. Maybe he's sick." I wanted to see for myself.

Manuel had a tidy duplex a few miles north of campus, where I shared a glass of wine with him once. I drove there and found a 'For Rent' sign out front. Peeking through a window, I saw an empty apartment.

Ray was confused and, I think, hurt by Manuel's disappearance. He invested a lot of time teaching him the finer details of the sign business to make him a more effective salesman. Ray genuinely liked him, too. Some days later, a friend of Ray's with a sign company across town, stopped by on business. During their visit, Ray described Manuel and his sudden departure.

"Why, that sounds like Pedro," his friend said, "He worked about six months and then vanished!" They matched notes a while longer and concluded it had to be the same man. I was nearby and heard all this, but kept my mouth shut.

I saw 'Soap is Cheap' in the stairway to The Loft, every day, and continued to ponder the Manuel story. Then one evening, he walked up those steps. "Rico!" he greeted me warmly. I might not have recognized him, passing on the street.

The pencil mustache was gone and he had a curly permanent. Impeccably dressed, as always, but transformed into a very modern disco look, with an open collar silk shirt.

"Manuel!" I said, "Have a seat and I'll get you a glass of wine."

"Roberto," he corrected me, rolling the 'R' dramatically. He followed me into the kitchen and showed me his spanking new driver license. It was issued in Nevada.

"How the hell do you do that?" I asked.

"It is not so difficult," he said, without offering any details. "I've been in Vegas, a place of never-ending sign work. But I had some loose ends here. Mind if I sleep on your couch tonight?"

We moved into the windowed front room with wine, cheese, and crackers. I knew I wouldn't get anywhere asking about his life story, so we had a chat about Ray and the sign crew instead.

"Yeah, that was a pretty nice job," Roberto said, "But I had to move on." He picked up the deck of cards on my trunk and started shuffling expertly. "There's another reason I wanted to see you," he said with a sly half-smile. "Probably wasting my breath, but I think you should come to Vegas with me for a while."

That was unexpected. "Why would I do that?" I asked.

"Yes, I'm painting signs," he sighed, "But with the rest of my time, I've carefully observed and figured out Las Vegas. The town is run and visited by a lot of people who aren't too bright. You and I are a couple of very smart guys. I have an *honest* scheme to make a pot of gold, but I need a partner." He tapped the cards on their side and set them on the table.

For me, Vegas would remain the road not taken. "Cut that deck and see what you get," I said.

He raised his eyebrows, but obliged, showing me the ten of spades.

"Jesus," I said, "That's the worst card in the deck! It's the same as the ten of swords in the Tarot." My Tarot book was also on the trunk. I found the page and showed it to him. It means failure, disaster, and, some believe, death.

Roberto took the book and looked over the description. "I thought you were bull shitting me, at first," he said, "That's quite a coincidence." He picked up the deck again and handed it to me. "You do it now, gypsy man, let's see what your card of the night is."

I shuffled them a while, a bit more clumsily than Roberto, set them on the table, and cut to the five of diamonds. If I hadn't already decided Vegas was out, that would have done it.

"Diamonds," Roberto said, thumbing through the book, "That's coins, I see." He found the page, read through the description, and slammed the book closed. "That's the poverty card!" he said, "This is some heavy duty shit, Rico."

He leaned back on the sofa and began petting Bagheera, who climbed on his lap. There was a gentle side to him, too. "So you're saying you don't want to go to Vegas." He said. "I doubted that you would."

"I'm saying," I started, "I'm *advising* that it's not a good idea for you either."

It was getting late. I got out a blanket and pillow for Roberto. "I'm going to sleep on that," he said, "Seriously, I'll give that some thought."

An early riser, like myself, Roberto joined me at dawn for scrambled eggs in the kitchen. The tree outside the window was full of birds singing. Curly came to the porch roof and chattered. I slid the window open a bit and stuck out a long wooden spoon with a dab of peanut butter on it. Curly cleaned it off.

"It's all clear to me now," Roberto said. "Las Vegas is no place for an hombre like you."

We shook hands and wished each other the best of luck. He assured me he would be cautious, looking out for that ten of spades. "I'm going to get a copy of the Tarot book," he said, "That might be a fun gig." On the way downstairs, he called up, laughing, "Soap is Cheap!"

I often wonder about Diego, Manuel, Pedro, or Roberto, but I never saw him again. Then again, he's the sort of guy who might still show up at my door, someday.

Nerves

I dreamed I was in pain and woke to find it so, perception and reality were one. My hands ached and my fingers weren't bending much. I sat up, fumbled with the light, and saw my fingers swollen like little hotdogs. Walking around The Loft, wiggling my fingers and moving my arms, brought my hands back to normal in ten minutes or so. What the hell was that? Sleep returned to me after a while with no further problems.

In the middle of the day, a week later, a sudden onset of pain hit me hard. I was in the sign shop darkroom and turned on the light. A painful white ring, like a dime size crater, had risen near the center of my right palm. With a finger of my left hand, I could feel it was a hard thing. Again, walking around the darkroom, moving my arm and fingers, made it go soft and melt back into my palm. That time, it was even more mystifying, like science fiction. It might not be an alien growing inside me, but something was most certainly wrong.

That evening, I visited Sid's brother, Dan, almost a doctor. He was pleased as hell to have a real patient and said he was gratified I had confidence in him. I didn't tell him he was my first stop because I knew I could see him right away and didn't think he'd send me a bill. I also thought it would eliminate a step, getting a knowledgeable referral to the right kind of doctor.

Dan got out his little black bag and gave me a general health exam. I was in good shape as far as he could tell without lab work, which he didn't have authority to order. My stated symptoms were bizarre and unheard of to him. He thought neurology was the best bet and gave me a name. But he said I should consider the possibility that my symptoms were psycho-somatically induced. What could I expect from a man on the road to psychiatry?

It took a few weeks to see the neurologist, during which time, both of my strange symptoms made repeat performances, putting my worry nerves on edge. Finally, my appointment came, and the doctor examined me, asking a lot of questions. He had heard a lot of crazy symptoms, but not mine.

The doctor gave me immediate advice, whether or not it was related to my problem. "Paints, thinners, and darkroom chemicals are very bad for you," he stated in as firm a way as he could. "They can kill you." I used gloves and tongs in the darkroom, but paint got on my skin daily. Lacquer thinner or acetone took it off quickly at the end of the day. "Your skin soaks that in very easily," he said, trying to get a strong message across, "And it's harming you." I left his office to give up many vials of blood for testing.

An EMG was also scheduled, that's electromyography, which tests the interaction of nerves and muscles. They laid me on a table, stuck electrodes all over me, including some on long needles shoved deep into my various muscles. Then they sent electric currents through me, while I flopped around the table like a freshly caught fish.

How did that feel, you ask? It was like deliberately standing up in the bath tub and touching the light switch. I knew what was coming each time the technician flipped the switch, but there was nothing I could do about it. It seemed to me that the test, itself, might be harmful to nerves. I was a wreck for a couple days.

At my follow-up appointment, I learned that the testing was negative for nerve damage and my blood looked fine. "But you need to take a complete break from paints and thinners to see if your symptoms stop," the doctor said, "If they do, you have to give them up."

Changes

In the sign shop office, I told Ray about my doctor's advice and described my weird symptoms. He didn't want to lose me and questioned the diagnosis. "I've worked with paint and thinners all my life," he declared, "And I feel fine!" Then he picked up his ever-present Maalox and took a slug from the bottle. I assured him I was unhappy about it, also, and offered to stick around to train a replacement.

Ray reluctantly put an ad in the paper the next day and, within a week, hired a bright young guy with photography experience. I worked another week, showing him the ropes.

When I explained my situation to Mark, he was saddened. "I understand," he signed, "But I will miss you."

I left the job amicably, with everyone, including The Brothers, wishing me the best of luck.

Since I left the job through no fault of my own, with written doctor's orders, I was eligible for unemployment benefits. A requirement for that is proof that you're looking for another position. I didn't want a job at that juncture, so I only applied for the ones I was obviously unqualified for.

I called Mom and Dad to tell them all this and they said they'd been hoping I would make more visits to help with picture framing. Their art gallery was continuing to grow. Some money from that and the unemployment check would get me by for a while.

A few days after the call home, my mailbox had a package from Dad. It was a vapor mask, elbow-length, industrial rubber gloves, and a letter. He thought it would be safe, with enclosed protection, to continue making my art prints, since it wasn't an all-day everyday activity. Thanks, Dad!

I had three art festivals coming up and wasn't completely prepared. When the first acceptance came, it was for the show I was doing with Tess. I thought we might have gotten in on the strength of *her* work. But then the two I was doing solo came through, giving me a confidence boost.

Tess made a lot of cute pen and inks, she thought might sell. I thought they'd also make great greeting cards. We picked out the best six, and I copied and screen-printed a few dozen cards of each. While I was at it, I made some larger prints of them.

One day we made a nice portfolio of our prints, put on nice clothes, and went to almost every gallery in the Columbus area. It took all day and we only sold two prints, which paid for dinner at Talita's Tacos. We sat in our usual booth by the window feeling exhausted. We agreed it was good to find out what *didn't work*. The art festival had to be better than that.

Postcard from Toledo

Tess and I were scheduled to share a booth at the Toledo Arts Fest, but there was a hitch. I could visit idol worship, but couldn't live with it. If I kept my feelings buried, it would only postpone their eventual eruption. She was unhappy and not understanding why I wanted to end the intimate part of our relationship. I did want a partner in life, and that was an impediment to finding one.

"We're still friends, though," she asked on the phone, a few weeks before the show, "aren't we?"

"Forever and always," I said, "I love you."

She didn't seem to understand me at all, but we got back to preparing for our exhibit.

My first festival experience was in the Cleveland area, earlier in the summer. I was a nervous wreck, so Mom went with me to boost my morale. The day was rainy and the show was moved to an ugly parking garage, adding to my stress. Somehow, I walked away with more money than I would have made in three weeks at the sign shop. That made Toledo look very important.

The Friday afternoon before the show, we drove north in my heavily loaded car and spent a fitful night in an extremely cheap hotel, not even getting what we paid for. At the show we were assigned a spot in a row of canopy spaces near the lakeshore.

Lucky Penny

There was music. A local band warmed up while we set up our booth. They played they're only national hit, *Post Card from Toledo*, several times. During the two days of the festival, we heard it another twenty times. It is indelibly etched on my memory. I could sing it right now, forty years later.

The festival opened and thousands of people arrived. I wanted to make a living with art, but the festival thing would take some getting used to. I don't like crowds. The booth space is our own little, self-designed niche, though, easing some of that discomfort. Then there are porta johns, not anyone's favorite bathroom venue. On hot summer days, I'm kind of a big air conditioning enthusiast. But we were selling our prints and originals.

Tess had her own issues. It was a long drive and a lot of work. The big crowd was partly about beer drinking and cotton candy, making the show site become trashy. She longed for a quiet place to meditate under a sheet in the middle of the afternoon. But, she too, was selling her prints.

"Are you having fun?" she asked, wearily, near the end of the first day.

I pulled some folding money out of my pocket. "This part is fun," I admitted. "I want to do twenty shows next year!"

With cash in our pockets, we found exponentially nicer accommodations that night, luxuriating in hot showers and watching an old movie in a big comfy bed. During the movie, Tess snuggled close and started writing on my chest with her finger. "I know you want to," she said.

"Gonna be friends, now," I said weakly.

"Yes, Ricky," she said, closing in on her objective, "We're *good* friends."

Lynne

Mom and Dad's gallery was still in a growing mode. I visited to help more frequently and not just on weekends, now that my time was more flexible. There was always a lot of picture framing work to do. I also helped customers pick artwork and design framing. Dad explained accounts and inventory, and I became familiar with the art they carried. They left me to run the place sometimes, and went off to walk in the park or go shopping.

Then I came up from Columbus and Mom and Dad were putting suitcases in their car. They thought they could escape for a few days, now that I could handle all phases of the business. The art gallery was a fun project, but the success of it tied them down, they confessed. "Maybe you'd consider working full time," they said, "There's plenty of work."

Northwood had become my home, and I didn't want to think about leaving that community. But I liked working in the gallery and began weighing the pros and cons. When I wasn't busy with customer work, I could be preparing for art festivals. The greater

Cleveland area had a lot of those. Then, thinking about returning to my home town turned me in another direction.

I got it in my head to look up my old friend who married Lynne. Maybe I was asking for trouble, but I called around and learned they had an apartment not too far away. On Sunday, when the gallery was closed, I drove there and found the address. No one was home, but I struck up a conversation with the guy in the next unit, sitting on his patio, and asked about his neighbors.

"It looks like he's living alone," he said, "I don't think they're together anymore."

I hurried back to Mom and Dad's and thumbed through the phonebook until I found the number for Lynne's parents. After a brief pep talk with myself, I called the number and Lynne answered!

Our conversation didn't get off to a good start. She thought I was yet, another classmate, calling about the ten year reunion, and she was not interested.

"No, no, no!" I said, "I'm the last person who would attend a reunion! Remember the sports rally study hall with Mr. Narcolepsy? We were always there." Lynne started to get the idea, and agreed to an afternoon date with me.

We went to the art museum, one of my favorite places. She looked great and I hoped I looked reasonably well groomed. We were a bit shy with each other at first, but then began filling each other in about the progress of our lives.

Lynne had been through some relationships gone sour and a failed marriage to an abusive spouse. She'd had a variety of jobs, held a degree from the community college, and lived in several different places around the country. Just then, she was taking a break, staying with her folks for a while to contemplate her next move.

We strolled through the museum and saw where our tastes meshed and where they didn't. In all it was a pleasant afternoon, more comfortable as it progressed. At the end of the day, I felt we still had that same rapport, liking and respecting each other. But I had no idea if she wanted to see me again. It was definitely premature to ask her to marry me.

I didn't call her the next day, but paced in front of the phone a few times. The day after that, she called me! I came over with a yellow rose in my hand. She gave me a lightning fast peck on the cheek and went off to find a vase. Then we went to the roller rink and had fun skating. In the evening, we slowly walked around our home town, remembering this place and that from our not so distant youth.

We came to a particular street corner that was very familiar. "I dreamed one night that you worked at this garage and changed my oil," I told her.

She laughed a moment, then met my eyes. "And now you're planning our future, aren't you?" she asked.

"Just the first chapter," I said, putting my arms around her gently. "The two of us will have to work out the rest together."

She looked surprised, but the smile was there and she returned my hug. "Forgive me if I need more than a few days to think about that," she said.

I told Lynne I had to go back to Columbus for a while, but would be back as soon as I could. The pros and cons of returning to the Erie lakeshore suddenly became simpler.

Northwood

In Columbus, I had a lot to do. My first stop was to see Tess and tell her I was moving north to work at my folk's art gallery. Then I braced myself. She was stunned for a moment, always hoping I'd see our relationship differently. Instead of writing on my chest, she gently hit it with her fists.

"Come and visit with some of your paintings and I'll frame them," I said.

"Yeah!" she brightened, "I'll do that." The fists became hands again.

"This means my apartment is available, if you want it," I added.

Then she really lit up. "That black ceiling is history!" She said, laughing.

"Bring some paint over this week and I'll help," I volunteered.

Lucky Penny

Back on Northwood, sadness swept over me. My life changed so much there, as did so many lives around me. I couldn't handle the thought of saying goodbye to these people and decided not to tell anyone, except Les and Jill. They were sorry to see me go, but liked Tess and looked forward to having her as their neighbor. They wondered if Bagheera was staying on with Tess, but I was taking her with me. I wanted to get her out of the city, so she could see what outdoor life was about.

I did spend some time visiting around the neighborhood, like I might any week. Sid was still with Jenny and still happy with it, but he had news.

"My brother is getting divorced!" he said.

"I thought Lulu would find someone else," I said, feeling vindicated.

"Yeah," Sid said, "Guess who?" He paused a long moment. "Lulu and *Max* are leaving for the Pacific Northwest!"

"Wow," I said, "No one would have predicted that!"

"And furthermore," Sid continued, "Dan is still in denial, acting like there isn't a knife in his heart. The man should be in counseling!"

Wednesday evening, I went to group therapy and started the session by telling them I was leaving town. I told them about the art gallery, finding Lynne, and choosing to move north.

"You're going to miss us," June said with a smile.

"And we're going to miss you," added Martha.

"You've explained your plans," George said, "But we didn't hear you share your feelings about all that."

"I'm excited, but sad, too," I said, "and a little frightened. I've been living in a great neighborhood. Northwood and the mental health center were safe and sheltering when I was at my low point. But as I slowly changed and grew, they were more like an incubator. Now, after taking a lot of small steps, I really think I'm ready to take a big one."

After our session, I got hugs from everyone and shed a few tears for another good thing I was leaving behind.

The week was mostly about packing and paint. My darkroom and books went into boxes. In the evenings, Tess came over to paint. The black, night sky, ceiling took two coats.

I wanted to load everything in my car the night before, still intending to sneak out of town. Les helped me carry down my trunk, guitar, and some boxes. It wasn't much more than I came with, a few years and a lifetime ago.

At dawn I put Bagheera in a perforated box and carried her down to my car. All was quiet on the street. I was uncertain of what lay ahead, but I knew what I was leaving: one of the most special times in my life and a place I would carry in my heart forever.

I looked up to see Carly at her attic window and we blew each other a kiss. Then I got in my car and drove slowly along Northwood for the last time.

Remembrance

Most of the old gang moved on from Northwood
shortly after I did,
but Carly still lives in her house there.

She moved back downstairs decades ago,
but once in a while
she slowly climbs the stairs to her attic.

In a chair by the window, she brews a pot of tea
 looking down on the ever-changing neighborhood,
always full of energetic new faces.

Then she sits back with her cup
and remembers a time when we, too,
embraced life with youthful vigor, passion,
and a thirst for self-discovery.

And she laughs.

Index